PARIS:

WITH

PEN AND PENCIL;

ITS

PEOPLE AND LITERATURE,

ITS

LIFE AND BUSINESS

BY

DAVID W. BARTLETT

AUTHOR OF "WHAT I SAW IN LONDON;" "LIFE OF LADY JANE GRAY;"
"LIFE OF JOAN OF ARC," ETC., ETC.

ILLUSTRATED.

NEW YORK:
HURST & CO., PUBLISHERS,
122 NASSAU STREET.

PREFACE.

The contents of this volume are the result of two visits to Paris. The first when Louis Napoleon was president of the Republic; and the second when Napoleon III. was emperor of France. I have sketched people and places as I saw them at both periods, and the reader should bear this in mind.

I have not endeavored to make a hand-book to Paris, but have described those places and objects which came more particularly under my notice. I have also thought it best, instead of devoting my whole space to the description of places, or the manners of the people — a subject which has been pretty well exhausted by other writers — to give a few sketches of the great men of Paris and of France; and among them, a few of the representative literary men of the past. There is not a general knowledge of French literature and authors, either past or present, among the mass of readers; and Paris and France can only be truly known through French authors and literature.

My object has been to add somewhat to the general reader's knowledge of Paris and the Parisians,—of the people and the place, whose social laws are the general guide of the civilized world.

CHURCH OF ST. SULSPICE.

CONTENTS.

CHAPTER XI.

CHAPTER XII.

WHAT I SAW IN PARIS.

CHAPTER I.

LONDON TO PARIS—HISTORY OF PARIS.

LONDON TO PARIS.

Few people now-a-days go direct to Paris from America. They land in Liverpool, get at least a birds-eye view of the country parts of England, stay in London a week or two, or longer, and then cross the channel for Paris.

The traveler who intends to wander over the continent, here takes his initiatory lesson in the system of passports. I first called upon the American minister, and my passport—made out in Washington—was *visé* for Paris. My next step was to hunt up the French consul, and pay him a dollar for affixing his signature to the precious document. At the first seaport this passport was taken from me, and a provisional one put into my keeping. At Paris the original one was returned! And this is a history of my passport between London and Paris, a distance traversed in a few hours. If such are the practices between two of the greatest and most civilized towns on the face of the earth, how unendurable must they be on the more despotic continent?

The summer was in its first month, and Paris was in its glory, and it was at such a time that I visited it. We took a steamer at the London bridge wharf for Boulogne,

The day promised well to be a boisterous one, but I had a very faint idea of the gale blowing in the channel. If I could have known, I should have waited, or gone by the express route, *via* Dover, the sea transit of which occupies only two hours. The fare by steamer from London to Boulogne was three dollars. The accommodations were meager, but the boat itself was a strong, lusty little fellow, and well fitted for the life it leads. I can easily dispense with the luxurious appointments which characterize the American steamboats, if safety is assured to me in severe weather.

The voyage down the Thames, was in many respects very delightful. Greenwich, Woolwich, Margate, and Ramsgate lie pleasantly upon this route. But the wind blew so fiercely in our teeth that we experienced little pleasure in looking at them. When we reached the channel we found it white with foam, and soon our little boat was tossed upon the waves like a gull. In my experience crossing the Atlantic, I had seen nothing so disagreeable as this. The motion was so quick and so continual, the boat so small, that I very soon found myself growing sick. The rain was disagreeable, and the sea was constantly breaking over the bulwarks. I could not stay below—the atmosphere was too stifling and hot. So I bribed a sailor to wrap about me his oil-cloth garments, and lay down near the engines with my face upturned to the black sky, and the sea-spray washing me from time to time. Such sea-sickness I never endured, though before I had sailed thousands of miles at sea, and have done the same since. From sundown till two o'clock the next morning I lay on the deck of the sloppy little boat, and when at last the Boulogne lights were to be seen, I was as heartily glad as ever in my life.

Thoroughly worn out, as soon as I landed upon the quay I handed my keys to a *commissaire*, gave up my passport, and sought a bed, and was soon in my dreams tossing again upon the channel-waves. I was waked by the *commissaire*, who entered my room with the keys. He had passed my baggage, got a provisional passport for me, and now very politely advised me to get up and take the first train to Paris, for I had told him I wished to be in Paris as soon as possible. Giving him a good fee for his trouble, and hastily quitting the apartment and paying for it, I was very soon in the railway station. My trunks were weighed, and I bought baggage tickets to Paris—price one sou. The first class fare was twenty-seven francs, or about five dollars, the distance one hundred and seventy miles. This was cheaper than first class railway traveling in England, though somewhat dearer than American railway prices.

The first class cars were the finest I have seen in any country—very far superior to American cars, and in many respects superior to the English. They were fitted up for four persons in each compartment, and a door opened into each from the side. The seat and back were beautifully cushioned, and the arms were stuffed in like manner, so that at night the weary traveler could sleep in them with great comfort.

The price of a third class ticket from Boulogne to Paris was only three dollars, and the cars were much better than the second class in America, and I noticed that many very respectably dressed ladies and gentlemen were in them—probably for short distances. It is quite common, both in England and France, in the summer, for people of wealth to travel by rail for a short distance by the cheapest class of cars.

I entered the car an utter stranger—no one knew me, and I knew no one. The language was unintelligible, for I found that to *read* French in America, is not to *talk* French in France. I could understand no one, or at least but a word here and there.

But the journey was a very delightful one. The country we passed through was beautiful, and the little farms were in an excellent state of cultivation. Flowers bloomed everywhere. There was not quite that degree of cultivation which the traveler observes in the best parts of England, but the scenery was none the less beantiful for that. Then, too, I saw everything with a romantic enthusiasm. It was the France I had read of, dreamed of, since I was a school-boy.

A gentleman was in the apartment who could talk English, having resided long in Boulogne, which the English frequent as a watering place, and he pointed out the interesting places on our journey. At Amiens we changed cars and stopped five minutes for refreshments. I was hungry enough to draw double rations, but I felt a little fear that I should get cheated, or could not make myself understood; but as the old saw has it, "Necessity is the mother of invention," and I satisfied my hunger with a moderate outlay of money. A few miles before we reached Paris, we stopped at the little village of Enghein, and it seemed to me that I never in my life had dreamed of so fairy-like a place. Beautiful lakes, rivers, fountains, flowers, and trees were scattered over the village with exquisite taste. To this place, on Sundays and holidays, the people of Paris repair, and dance in its cheap gardens and drink cheap wines.

When we reached Paris my trunks were again searched and underwent a short examination, to see that no wines or provisions were concealed in them. A tax is laid upon all such articles when they enter the city, and this is the reason why on Sunday the people flock out of town to enjoy their *fêtes*. In the country there are no taxes on wine and edibles, and as a matter of economy they go outside of the walls for their pleasure.

When my baggage was examined, I took an omnibus to the hotel Bedford, Rue de l'Arcade, where I proposed to stay but a few days, until I could hunt up permanent apartments. My room was a delightful one and fitted up in elegant style. I was in the best part of Paris. Two minutes walk away were the *Champs Elysees*—the Madeleine church, the Tuileries, etc., etc. But I was too tired to go out, and after a French dinner and a lounge in the reading-room, I went to sleep, and the next morning's sun found me at last entirely recovered from my wretched passage across the channel.

My second trip to Paris was in many respects different from the first—which I have just described. The route was a new one, and pleasanter than that *via* Boulogne. Our party took an express train from the London bridge terminus for Newhaven, a small sea-port. The cars were fitted up with every comfort, and we made the passage in quick time. At three P. M. we went on board a little steamer for Dieppe, where we arrived at nine o'clock. After a delay of an hour we entered a railway carriage fitted up in a very beautiful and luxurious style. At Dieppe we had no trouble with our passports, keeping the originals, and simply showing them to the custom-house officials. Our ride to Paris was in the night, yet was very comfortable.

In coming back to London, we made the trip to Dieppe in the daytime, and found it to be very beautiful. From

Paris to Rouen the railway runs a great share of the way in sight of the river Seine, and often upon its banks. Many of the views from the train were romantic, and some of them wildly grand. Upon the whole, this route is the pleasantest between Paris and London, as it is one of the cheapest. There is one objection, however, and that is the length of the sea voyage—six hours. Those who dislike the water will prefer the Dover route.

HISTORY OF PARIS.

The origin of Paris is not known. According to certain writers, a wandering tribe built their huts upon the island now called *la Cité*. This was their home, and being surrounded by water, it was easily defended against the approach of hostile tribes. The name of the place was Lutetia, and to themselves they gave the name of *Parisii*, from the Celtic word *par*, a frontier or extremity

This tribe was one of sixty-four which were confederated, and when the conquest of Gaul took place under Julius Cæsar, the *Parisii* occupied the island. The ground now covered by Paris was either a marsh or forest, and two bridges communicated from the island to it. The islanders were slow to give up their Druidical sacrifices, and it is doubtful whether the Roman gods ever were worshiped by them, though fragments of an altar of Jupiter have been found under the choir of the cathedral of Notre Dame. Nearly four hundred years after Christ, the Emperor Julian remodeled the government and laws of Gaul and Lutetia, and changed its name to *Parisii*. It then, too, became a city, and had considerable trade. For five hundred years Paris was under Roman domination. A palace was erected for municipal purposes in the city, and another on the south bank of the Seine, the remains of which can still be seen. The Roman emperors frequently resided in this palace while waging war with the northern barbarians. Constantine and Constantius visited it; Julian spent three winters in it; Valentian and Gratian also made it a temporary residence.

The monks have a tradition that the gospel was first preached in Paris about the year 250, by St. Denis, and that he suffered martyrdom at Montmartre. A chapel was early erected on the spot now occupied by Notre Dame. In 406 the northern barbarians made a descent upon the Roman provinces, and in 445 Paris was stormed by them. Before the year 500 Paris was independent of the Roman domination. Clovis was its master, and marrying Clotilde, he embraced christianity and erected a church. The island was now surrounded by walls and had gates. The famous church of St. German L'Auxerrois was built at this time. For two hundred and fifty years, Paris retrograded rather than advanced in civilization, and the refinements introduced by the Romans were nearly forgotten. In 845 the Normans sacked and burnt Paris. Still again it was besieged, but such was the valor of its inhabitants that the enemy were glad to raise the siege. Hugues Capet was elected king in 987, and the crown became hereditary. In his reign the Palace of Justice was commenced. Buildings were erected on all sides, and new streets were opened. Under Louis le Gros the Louvre was rebuilt, it having existed since the time of Dagobert. Bishop Sully began the foundations of Notre Dame in 1163, and about that time the Knights Templars erected a palace.

Under the reign of Philip Augustus many of the public edifices were embellished and new churches and towers were built. In 1250 Robert Serbon founded schools—a hospital and school of surgery were also about this time commenced.

Under Charles V. the city flourished finely, and the Bastille and the Palace de Tourvelles were erected. The Louvre also was repaired. Next came the unhappy reign of Charles VI., who was struck with insanity. In 1421 the English occupied Paris, but under Charles VII. they were driven from it and the Greek language was taught for the first time in the University of Paris. It had then twenty-five thousand students. Under the reign of successive monarchs Paris was, from famine and plague, so depopulated that its gates were thrown open to the malefactors of all countries. In 1470 the art of printing was introduced into the city and a post-office was established. In the reign of Francis I. the arts and literature sprang into a new life. The heavy buildings called the Louvre were demolished, and a new palace commenced upon the old site. In 1533 the Hotel de Ville was begun, and many fine buildings were erected. The wars of the sects, or rather religions, followed, and among them occurred the terrible St. Bartholomew massacre. Henry IV. brought peace to the kingdom and added greatly to the beauty and attractiveness of Paris.

Under Louis XIII. several new streets were opened, and the Palais Royal and the palace of the Luxembourg begun. Under the succeeding king the wars of the Fronde occurred, but the projects of the preceding king were carried out, and more than eighty new streets were opened. The planting of trees in the Champs Elysees, also took place under the reign of Louis XIV. The palace of the Tuileries was enlarged, the Hotel des Invalides, a foundling hospital, and several bridges were built.

Louis XV. established the manufactory of porcelain at Sevres, and also added much to the beauty of Paris. He commenced the erection of the Madeleine. Theaters and comic opera-houses were speedily built, and water was distributed over the city by the use of steam-engines.

Then broke out the revolution, and many fine monuments were destroyed. But it was under the Directory that the Museum of the Louvre was opened, and under Napoleon the capital assumed a splendor it had never known before. Under the succeeding kings it continued to increase in wealth and magnificence, until it is unquestionably the finest city in the world.

I have now in a short space given the reader a preliminary sketch of Paris, and will proceed at once to describe what I saw in it, and the impressions I received, while a resident in that city.

CHAPTER II.

RESTAURANTS—A WALK AND GOSSIP.

Boulevard du Temple.

RESTAURANTS, CAFES, ETC.

THE first thing the stranger does in Paris, is of course to find temporary lodging, and the next is to select a good *restaurant*. Paris without its *restaurants*, *cafés*, *estaminets*, and *cercles*, would be shorn of half its glory. They are one of its most distinguished and peculiar features. Between the hours of five and eight, in the evening of course, all Paris is in those *restaurants*. The scene at such times is enlivening in the highest degree. The Boulevards contain the finest in the city, for there nearly all the first-class saloons are kept. There are retired streets in which are kept houses on the same plan, but

PARIS & ARCH OF TRIUMPH.

with prices moderate in the extreme. You can go on the Boulevards and pay for a breakfast, if you choose, fifty or even sixty francs, or you can retire to some quiet spot and pay one franc for your frugal meal. It is of course not common for any one to pay the largest sum named, but there are persons in Paris who do it, young men who with us are vulgarly denominated "swells," and who like to astonish their friends by their extravagance.

Out of curiosity I went one day with a friend to one of the most gorgeous of the *restaurants* on the Boulevards. Notwithstanding the descriptions I had read and listened to from the lips of friends, I was surprised at the splendor and style of the place. We sat down before a fine window which was raised, looking into the street. Indeed, so close sat we to it that the fashionable promenaders could each, if he liked, have peeped into our dishes. But Parisians never trouble strangers with their inquisitiveness. We sat down before a table of exquisite marble, and a waiter dressed as neatly, and indeed gracefully, as a gentleman, handed us a bill of fare. It was long enough in itself to make a man a dinner, if the material were only palatable. Including dessert and wines, there were one hundred specifications! There were ten kinds of meat, and fourteen varieties of poultry. Of course there were many varieties of game, and there were eight kinds of pastry. Of fish there were fourteen kinds, there were ten side dishes, a dozen sweet dishes, and a dozen kinds of wine.

The elegance of the apartment can scarcely be imagined, and the savory smell which arose from neighboring tables occupied by fashionable men and women, invited us to a repast. We called, however, but for a dish or two, and after we had eaten them, we had coffee, and over our cups gazed out upon the gay scene before us. It was novel, indeed, to the American eye, and we sat long and discussed it. In this *restaurant* there were private rooms, called *Cabinets de Societe*, and into them go men and women at all hours, by day and night. It is also a common sight to see the public apartments of the *restaurants* filled with people of both sexes. Ladies sit down even in the street with gentlemen, to sup chocolate or lemonade. There is not much eaves-dropping in Paris, and you can do as you please, nor fear curious eyes nor scandal-loving tongues. This is very different from London. There, if you do anything out of the common way, you will be stared at and talked about. *There*, if you take a lady into a public eating-house, *her* position, at least, will not be a very pleasant one.

There are many places in the Palais Royal, the basement floor of which, fronting upon the court of the palace, is given up to shops, where for two or three francs a dinner can be purchased which will consist of soup, two dishes from a large list at choice, a dessert, and bread and wine. There are places, indeed, where for twenty-five sous a dinner sufficient to satisfy one's hunger can be purchased, but I must confess that while in Paris I could never yet make up my mind to patronize a cheap *restaurant*. I knew too well, by the tales of more experienced Parisians, the shifts to which the cook of one of these cheap establishments is sometimes reduced to produce an attractive dish. The material sometimes would not bear a close examination—much less the *cuisine*.

I was astonished to see the quantities of bread devoured by the frequenters of the eating-houses, but I soon equaled my neighbors. Paris bread is the best in the world, or at least, it is the most palatable I ever tasted

JARDIN DU PALAIS ROYAL.

It is made in rolls six feet long, and sometimes I have seen it eight feet long. Before now, I have seen a couple dining near the corner of a room, with their roll of bread thrown like a cane against the wall, and as often as they wanted a fresh slice, the roll was very coolly brought over and decapitated. The Frenchman eats little meat, but enormously of the staff of life. The chocolate and coffee which are to be had in the French *cafés*, are very delicious, and though after a fair and long trial I never could like French cookery as well as the English, yet I would not for a moment pretend that any cooks in the world equal those of Paris in the art of imparting exquisite flavor to a dish. It is quite common for the French to use brandy in their coffee.

People who take apartments in Paris often prefer to have their meals sent to their private rooms, and by a special bargain this is done by any of the restaurants, but more especially by a class of houses called *traiteurs*, whose chief business is to furnish cooked dishes to families in their own homes. In going to a hotel in Paris, the stranger never feels in the slightest degree bound to get his meals there. He hires his room and that is all, and goes where he pleases. The *cafés* are in the best portions of the town, magnificent places, often exceeding in splendor the restaurants. They furnish coffee, chocolate, all manner of ices and fruits, and cigars. At these places one meets well-dressed ladies, and more than once in them I have seen well-dressed women smoking cigarettos. Love intrigues are carried on at these places, for a Paris lady can easily steal from her home to such a place under cover of the night. A majority, however, of the women to be seen at such places, are those who have no position in society, the wandering nymphs of the night, or the poor grisettes. It is not strange that the poor shop-girl is easily attracted to such gorgeous places by men far above her in station.

Outside of all the cafés little tables are placed on the pavement, with chairs around them. These places are delightful in the summer evenings, and are always crowded. A promenade through some of the best streets of a summer night is a brilliant spectacle, and more like a promenade through a drawing-room than through an American street. The proprietors of those places do not intend to keep restaurants, but quite a variety of food, hot or cold, is always on hand, and wines of all kinds are sold.

I well remember my first visit to a French *café*. It was when Louis Napoleon was president, not emperor of France, and when there was more liberty in Paris than there is now. I dropped into one near the Boulevards, which, while it contained everything which could add to one's comfort, still was not one of the first class. Several officers were dining in it, and in some way I came in contact with one of them in such a manner that he discovered I was an American. At once his conduct toward me was of the most cordial kind, and his fellows rose and bade me welcome to France. The simple fact that I was a republican from America aroused the enthusiasm of all. I found, afterward, that the regiment to which these officers belonged was suspected by the president of being democratic in its sympathies.

The reading-rooms of Paris are one of its best institutions. They are scattered all over the city, but the best is Galignani's, which contains over twenty thousand volumes in all languages. The subscription price for a month is eight francs, for a fortnight five francs, and for a day ten sous.

There are reading-rooms furnished only with newspapers, where for a small sum of money one can read the papers. These places are few in comparison with their numbers in the days of the republic, however. Under the despotic rule of Louis Napoleon, the newspaper business has drooped.

An anonymous writer in one of Chambers' publications, tells a good story, and it is a true one, of Père Fabrice, who amassed a fortune in Paris. The story is told as follows:

"He had always a turn for speculation, and being a private soldier he made money by selling small articles to his fellow soldiers. When his term of service had expired, he entered the employ of a rag-merchant, and in a little while proposed a partnership with his master, who laughed at his impudence. He then set up an opposition shop, and lost all he had saved in a month. He then became a porter at the *halles* where turkeys were sold. He noticed that those which remained unsold, in a day or two lost half their value. He asked the old women how the customers knew the turkeys were not fresh. They replied that the legs changed from a bright black to a dingy brown. Fabrice went home, was absent the next day from the *halles*, and on the third day returned with a bottle of liquid. Seizing hold of the first brown-legged turkey he met with, he forthwith painted its legs out of the contents of his bottle, and placing the thus decorated bird by the side of one just killed, he asked who now was able to see the difference between the fresh bird and the stale one? The old women were seized with admiration. They are a curious set of beings, those *dames de la halle;* their admiration is unbounded for successful adventurers—witness their enthusiasm for Louis Napoleon. They adopted our friend's idea without hesitation, made an agreement with him on the principle of the division of profits; and it immediately became a statistical puzzle with the curious inquirers on these subjects, how it came to pass that stale turkeys should have all at once disappeared from the Paris market? It was set down to the increase of prosperity consequent on the constitutional *régime* and the wisdom of the citizen-king. The old women profited largely; but unfortunately, like the rest of the world, they in time forgot both their enthusiasm and their benefactor, and Père Fabrice found himself involved in a daily succession of squabbles about his half-profits. Tired out at last, he made an arrangement with the old dames, and, in military phrase, sold out. Possessed now of about double the capital with which he entered, he recollected his old friend, the rag-merchant, and went a second time to propose a partnership. 'I am a man of capital now,' he said; 'you need not laugh so loud this time.' The rag-merchant asked the amount of his capital; and when he heard it, whistled *Ninon dormait*, and turned upon his heel. 'No wonder,' said Fabrice afterward; 'I little knew then what a rag-merchant was worth. That man could have bought up two of Louis Philippe's ministers of finance.' At the time, however, he did not take the matter so philosophically, and resolved, after the fashion of his class, not to drown himself, but to make a night of it. He found a friend, and went with him to dine at a small eating-house. While there, they noticed the quantity of broken bread thrown under the tables by the reckless and quarrelsome set that frequented the place; and his friend remarked, that if all the bread so thrown about were collected, it would feed half the *quartier*. Fabrice said nothing; but he was in search of an idea, and he took up his friend's. The next day, he called on the restaurateur, and asked him for what he would sell the broken bread he was accustomed to sweep in the dust-pan. The bread he wanted, it should be observed, was a very different thing from the fragments left upon the table; these had been consecrated to the marrow's soup from time immemorial. He wanted the dirty bread actually thrown under the table, which even a Parisian restaurateur of the Quartier Latin, whose business it was to collect dirt and crumbs, had hitherto thrown away. Our restaurateur caught eagerly at the offer, made a bargain for a small sum; and Master Fabrice forthwith proceeded to about a hundred eating-houses of the same kind, with all of whom he made similar bargains. Upon this he established a bakery, extending his operations till there was scarcely a restaurant in Paris of which the sweepings did not find their way to the oven of Père Fabrice. Hence it is that the fourpenny restaurants are supplied; hence it is that the itinerant venders of gingerbread find their first material. Let any man who eats bread at any very cheap place in the capital take warning, if his stomach goes against the idea of a *réchauffé* of bread from the dust-hole. Fabrice, notwithstanding some extravagances with the fair sex, became a millionaire; and the greatest glory of his life was—that he lived to eclipse his old master, the rag-merchant."

The same writer also gives a graphic description of one class of restaurants in Paris—the pot-luck shops:

"Pot-luck, or the *fortune de pot*, is on the whole the most curious feeding spectacle in Europe. There are more than a dozen shops in Paris where this mode of procuring a dinner is practiced, chiefly in the back streets abutting on the Pantheon. About two o'clock, a parcel of men in dirty blouses, with sallow faces, and an indescribable mixture of recklessness, jollity, and misery—strange as the juxtaposition of terms may seem—lurking about their eyes and the corners of their mouths, take their seats in a room where there is not the slightest appearance of any preparation for food, nothing but half-a-dozen old deal-tables, with forms beside them, on the side of the room, and one large table in the middle. They pass away the time in vehement gesticulation, and talking in a loud tone; so much of what they say is in *argot*, that the stranger will not find it easy to comprehend them. He would think they were talking crime or politics—not a bit of it; their talk is altogether about their mistresses. Love and feeding make up the existence of these beings; and we may judge of the quality of the former by what we are about to see of the latter. A huge bowl is at last introduced, and placed on the table in the middle of the room. At the same time a set of basins, corresponding to the number of the guests, are placed on the side-tables. A woman, with her nose on one side, good eyes, and the thinnest of all possible lips, opening every now and then to disclose the white teeth which garnish an enormous mouth, takes her place before it. She is the presiding deity of the temple; and there is not a man present to whom it would not be the crowning felicity of the moment to obtain a smile from features so little used to the business of smiling, that one wonders how they would set about it if the necessity should ever arise. Every cap is doffed with a grim politeness peculiar to that class of humanity, and a series of compliments fly into the face of Madame Michel, part leveled at her eyes, and part at the laced cap, in perfect taste, by which those eyes are shrouded. Mère Michel, however, says nothing in return, but proceeds to stir with a thick ladle, looking much larger than it really is, the contents of the bowl before her. These contents are an enormous quantity of thick brown liquid, in the midst of which swim numerous islands of vegetable matter and a few pieces of meat. Meanwhile, a damsel, hideously ugly—but whose ugliness is in part concealed by a neat, trim cap—makes the tour of the room with a box of tickets, grown black by use, and numbered from one to whatever number may be that of the company. Each of them gives four sous to this Hebe of the place, accompanying the action with an amorous look, which is both the habit and the duty of every Frenchman when he has anything to do with the opposite sex, and which is not always a matter of course, for Marie has her admirers, and has been the cause of more than one *rixe* in in the Rue des Anglais. The tickets distributed, up rises number one—with a joke got ready for the occasion, and a look of earnest anxiety, as if he were going to throw for a kingdom—takes the ladle, plunges it into the bowl, and transfers whatever it brings up to his basin. It is contrary to the rules for any man to hesitate when he has once made his plunge, though he has a perfect right to take his time in a previous survey of the *ocean*—a privilege of which he always avails himself. If he brings up one of the pieces of meat, the glisten of his eye and the applauding murmur which goes round the assembly give him a momentary exultation, which it is difficult to conceive by those who have not witnessed it. In this the spirit of successful gambling is, beyond all doubt, the uppermost feeling; it mixes itself up with everything done by that class of society, and is the main reason of the popularity of these places with their *habitués;* for when the customers have once acquired the habit, they rarely go anywhere else."

Omnibus.

A WALK AND GOSSIP.

One of my first days in Paris I sauntered out to find some American newspapers, that I might know something of what had transpired in America for weeks previous. I directed my steps to the office of Messrs. Livingston, Wells & Co., where I had been informed a reading-room was always kept open for the use of American strangers in Paris. The morning was a delightful one, and I could but contrast it with the usual weather of London. During months of residence in the English metropolis I had seen no atmosphere like this, and my spirits, like the sky, were clear and bright.

On my way I saw a novel sight, and to me the first intimation that the people of Paris, so widely famed for their politeness, refinement, and civilization, are yet addicted to certain practices for which the wildest barbarian in the far west would blush. I saw men in open day, in the open walk, which was crowded with women as well as men, commit nuisances of a kind I need not particularize but which seemed to excite neither wonder nor disgust in the by-passers. Indeed I saw they were quite accustomed to such sights, and their nonchalance was only equaled by that of the well-dressed gentlemen who were the guilty parties. I very soon learned more of Paris, and found that not in this matter alone were its citizens deficient in refinement, but in still weightier matters.

I soon reached the American reading-room, and walked in. My first act was to look at the register where all persons who call inscribe their names, and I was surprised to notice the number of Americans present in Paris. It only proved what I long had heard, that Americans take more naturally to the French than to the sturdy, self-sufficient Englishman. As it is in the matter of fashions, so it is regarding almost everything else, save morals, and I doubt if the tone of fashionable society in New York is any better than in Paris.

I was heartily rejoiced to take an American newspaper in my hand again. There were the clear open face of the plain-spoken *Tribune*, the sprightly columns of the *Times*, and the more dignified columns of the Washington journals. There were also many other familiar papers on the table, and they were all touched before I left. It was like a cool spring in the wide desert. For I confess that I love the newspaper, if it only be of the right sort. From early habit, I cannot live without it. Let any man pursue the vocation of an editor for a few years, and he will find it difficult, after, to live without a good supply of newspapers, and they must be of the old-fashioned home kind.

I did not easily accustom myself to the Paris journals. Cheap enough some of them were, but still the strange language was an obstacle. They are worse printed than ours, and are by no means equal to such journals as the *Times* and *Tribune.* They publish continued stories, or novels, and racy criticisms of music, art, and literature. The political department of the French newspaper at the present day is the weakest part of the sheet. It is lifeless. A few meager facts are recorded, and there is a little tame comment, and that is all. There was a time when the political department of a French newspaper was its most brilliant feature. During the exciting times which presaged the downfall of Louis Philippe, and also during the early days of the republic, the Paris press was in the full tide of success, and was exceedingly brilliant. The daily journals abounded, and their subscription lists were enormous. Where there is freedom, men and women *will* read—and where there is unmitigated despotism, the people care little to read the sickly journals which are permitted to drag out an existence.

There is one journal published in Paris in the English language, "*Galignani's Messenger.*" It is old, and in its way is very useful, but it is principally made up of extracts from the English journals. It has no editorial ability or originality, and of course never advances any opinion upon a political question.

On my return home I passed through a street often mentioned by Eugene Sue in his Mysteries of Paris—a street formerly noted for the vile character of its inhabitants. It was formerly filled with robbers and cut-throats, and even now I should not care to risk my life in this street after midnight, with no policemen near. It is exceedingly narrow, for I stood in the center and touched with the tips of my fingers the walls of both sides of the street. It is very dark and gloomy, and queer-looking passages run up on either side from the street. Some of them were frightful enough in their appearance. To be lost in such a place in the dead of night, even now, would be no pleasant fate, for desperate characters still haunt the spot. Possibly the next morning, or a few mornings after, the stranger's body might be seen at *La Morgue*. That is the place where all dead bodies found in the river or streets are exhibited—suicides and murdered men and women.

Talking of this street and its reputation in Eugene Sue's novels, reminds me of the man. When I first saw it he had just been elected to the Chamber of Deputies by an overwhelming majority. It was not because Sue was the favorite candidate of the republicans, but he stood in such a position that his defeat would have been considered a government victory, and consequently he was elected. I was glad to find the man unpopular among democrats of Paris, for his life, like his books, has many pages in it that were better not read. At that time he was living very quietly in a village just out of Paris, and though surrounded with voluptuous luxuries, he was in his life strictly virtuous. He was the same afterward, and being very wealthy, gave a great deal to the poor. His novels are everywhere read in France.

I was not a little surprised during my first days in Paris to see the popularity of Cooper as a novelist. His stories are for sale at every book-stall, and are in all the libraries. They are sold with illustrations at a cheap rate, and I think I may say with safety that he is as widely read in France as any foreign novelist. This is a little singular when it is remembered how difficult it is to convey the broken Indian language to a French reader. This is one of the best features of Cooper's novels—the striking manner in which he portrays the language of the North

American Indian and his idiomatic expressions. Yet such is the charm of his stories that they have found their way over Europe. The translations into the French language must be good.

Another author read widely in Paris, as she is all over Europe, is Mrs. Stowe. *Uncle Tom* is a familiar name in the brilliant capital of France, and even yet his ideal portraits hang in many shop windows, and the face of Mrs. Stowe peeps forth beside it. *Uncle Tom's Cabin* was wonderfully popular among all classes, and to very many—what a fact!—it brought their first idea of Jesus Christ as he is delineated in the New Testament. But Mrs. Stowe's *Sunny Memories* was very severely criticised and generally laughed at—especially her criticisms upon art.

Walking one evening in the Champs Elysees, I found a little family of singers from the Alps, underneath one of the large trees. You should have heard them sing their native songs, so plaintive and yet so mild. Father and mother, two little sisters and a brother, were begging their bread in that way. They were dressed very neatly, although evidently extremely poor. The father had a violin which he played very sweetly, the mother sang, the two little girls danced, and the boy put in a soft and melancholy tenor. I hardly ever listened to sadder music. It seemed as if their hearts were in it, saddened at the thought of exile from their native mountains. After singing for a long time, they stopped and looked up appealingly to the crowd—but not a sou fell to the ground. Once more they essayed to sing, with a heavier sorrow upon their faces, for they were hungry and had no bread. They stopped again—not a solitary sou was given to them. A large tear rolled down the cheek of the father—you should have seen the answering impulse of the crowd—how the sous rattled upon the ground. They saw instantly that it was no common beggar before them, but one who deserved their alms. At once, as if a heaven full of clouds had divided and the sunshine flashed full upon their faces, the band of singers grew radiant and happy. Such is life—a compound of sorrow and gayety.

The Parisian omnibus system is the best in the world, and I found it very useful and agreeable always while wandering over the city. The vehicles are large and clean, and each passenger has a chair fastened firmly to the sides of the carriage. Six sous will carry a person anywhere in Paris, and if two lines are necessary to reach the desired place, a ticket is given by the conductor of the first omnibus, which entitles the holder to another ride in the new line. The omnibus system is worked to perfection only in Paris, and is there a great blessing to people who cannot afford to drive their own carriages.

THE BOURSE—GALIGNANI'S, ETC., ETC.

The Paris Exchange is on the Rue Vivienne, and is approached from the Tuileries from that street or *via* the Palais National, and a succession of the most beautiful arcade-shops in Paris or the world. If the day be rainy, the stranger can thread his way to it under the long arcades as dry as if in his own room at the hotel. I confess to a fondness for wandering though such places as these arcades, where the riches of the shops are displayed in their large windows. In America it is not usual to fill the windows of stores full of articles with the price of each attached, but it is always so in London and Paris. A jewelry store will exhibit a hundred kinds of watches with their different prices attached, and the different shops will display what they contain in like manner. There are, too, in Paris and London places called "Curiosity shops." The first time I ever saw one of these shops with its green windows and name over the door, memory instantly recalled a man never to be forgotten. Will any one who has read Charles Dickens ever forget his "Curiosity Shop," the old grandfather and little Nell? When I entered the shop—the windows filled with old swords, pistols, and stilettos—it seemed to me that I must meet the old gray-haired man, or gentle Nell, or the ugly Quilp and Dick Swiveller. But they were not there.

Palais de la Bourse.

But I have been stopping in a curiosity shop when I should be on my way to the Bourse. The Paris Bourse, or Exchange, is perhaps the finest building of its kind on the continent. Its magnificence is very properly of the most solid and substantial kind. For should not the exchange for the greatest merchants of Paris be built in a stable rather than in a slight and beautiful manner? The form of the structure is that of a parallelogram, and it is two hundred and twelve by one hundred and twenty-six feet. It is surrounded by sixty-six Corinthian columns, which support an entablature and a worked attic. It is approached by a flight of steps which extend across the whole western front. Over the western entrance is the following inscription—BOURSE ET TRIBUNAL DE COMMERCE. The roof is made of copper and iron. The hall in the center of the building where the merchants meet is very large—one hundred and sixteen feet long and seventy-six feet broad. Just below the cornice are inscribed the names of the principal cities in the world, and over the middle arch there is a clock, which on an opposite dial-plate marks the direction of the wind out of doors.

The hall is lighted from the roof—the ceiling is covered with fine paintings, or as they are styled "monochrane drawings." Europe, Asia, Africa, and America are represented in groups. In one, the city of Paris is represented as delivering her keys to the God of Commerce, and inviting Commercial Justice to enter the walls prepared for her.

The hall is paved with a fine marble, and two thousand persons can be accommodated upon the central floor. There is a smaller inclosure at the east end, where the merchants and stockholders transact their daily business. The hours are from one o'clock to three for the public stocks, and till half past five for all others. The public is allowed to visit the Bourse from nine in the morning till five at night. A very singular regulation exists in reference to the ladies. No woman is admitted into the Bourse without a special order from the proper authorities. The cause for this is the fact that years ago, when ladies were admitted to the Bourse, they became very much addicted to gambling there, and also enticed the gentlemen into similar practices. It is not likely that the old stockholders were tempted into any vicious practices, but the presence of women was enough to attract another class of men—idlers and fashionable gamblers—until the exchange was turned into a-gambling-saloon. The matter was soon set to rights when women were shut out.

Paris was formerly without an Exchange, and the merchants held their meetings in an old building which John Law, the celebrated financier, once occupied. They afterward met in the Palais Royal, and still later, in a comparatively obscure street. The first stone of the Bourse was laid on the 28th of March, 1808, and the works proceeded with dispatch till 1814, when they were suspended. It was completed in 1826. The architect who designed it died when it was half completed, but the plan was carried out, though by a new architect. It is now a model building of its kind, and cost nearly nine millions of francs. In comprehensive magnificence it has no rival in Paris—perhaps not in the world. The Royal Exchange of London, though a fine building, is a pigmy beside this massive and colossal structure. The best view can be obtained from the Rue Vivienne. From this street one has a fine view of the fine marble steps ascending to it, and which stretch completely across the western part.

The history of all the great panics which have been experienced on the Paris Exchange would be an excellent history of the fortunes of France. The slightest premonition of change is felt at once at the Bourse, and as each successive revolution has swept over the country, it has written its history in ineffaceable characters on Change. Panic has followed panic, and the stocks fly up or down according to the views outside. The breath of war sets all its interests into a trembling condition, and an election, before now, has sent the thrill to the very center of that grand old money-palace.

On my way home from the Bourse, I stopped to go over Galignani's Reading Room. It is a capital collection of the best books of all countries, some of them in French, some in English, and others in German. I found on the shelves many American republications, but Cooper was always first among these. For a small sum the stranger can subscribe to this library, either for a month or a year, and supply himself with reading and the newspapers of the world.

The Messrs. Galignani publish an English journal in Paris. It is a daily, and has no opinions of its own. Of course, an original and independent journal could not be allowed to exist in Paris.

For this reason *Galignani's Messenger* is a vapid concern. It presents no thoughts to the reader. It is interesting to the Englishman in Paris, because it gathers English news, and presents it in the original language. As there are always a great many Englishmen in Paris, the journal is tolerably well supported. Then, again, the Paris shop-keepers and hotel-owners know very well that the English are among their best customers, and they advertise largely in it. So far as my experience has gone, I have found the *Messenger* quite unfair to America. It quotes from the worst of American journals, and is sure to parade anything that may be for the disadvantage of American reputation. It also is generally sure of showing by its quotations its sympathy with "the powers that be." This may all be natural enough, for it is for their interest to stand well with the despot who rules France, but to an American, and a republican, it excites only disgust. At present the *Messenger* is as good, or nearly so, as any of the French journals, but when the latter had liberty to write as they pleased, the contrast between the French and English press in Paris was ludicrous. In one you had fearless political writing, wit, and spice. In the other, nothing but selections.

Once, while in Paris, during the days of the republic, I called upon the editor of one of the prominent French journals. It was a journal which had again and again paid government fines for the utterance of its honest sentiments, both under Louis Philippe and the presidency of Louis Napoleon. Before the revolution it had a very great influence over the people, and in the days of the so-called republic. The struggle between it and the government, at that time was continued. Its editor's great aim was to express as much truth as was possible and escape the government fine, which in the end would suppress the journal.

As I entered the building in which this journal was printed and published, I felt a kind of awe creeping over me, as if coming into the presence of a great mind. We entered the editor's office; a little green baize-covered table by a window, pen and ink, and scissors, indicated the room. One might indeed tremble in such a place. What greater place is there in this world than an editor's office, if his journal be one which sells by tens of thousands and sways a vast number of intelligent men? A throne-room is nothing in comparison to it. Thrones are demolished by the journals. Especially in Paris has such been the case. The liberal press has in past years con trolled the French people to a wonderful extent. Kings and queens have physical power, but here in this little room was the throne-room of intellect. A door opened out of it into the printing-room, where the thoughts were stamped upon paper, afterward to be impressed upon a hundred thousand minds.

The editor sat over his little desk, an earnest, care-worn, yet hopeful man. His fingers trembled with nervousness, yet his eye was like an eagle's. He did not stir when we first entered, did not even see us, he was so deeply absorbed in what lay before him upon his table. I was glad to watch him for a moment, unobserved. He was no fashionable editor, made no play of his work. He felt the responsibility of his position, and endeavored honestly to do his duty. His forehead was high, his eye black, and his face was very pale. Suddenly he looked up and saw us, and recognized my friend. It was enough that I was a republican, from America, and unlike some Americans, abated not a jot of my radicalism when in foreign countries.

I looked around the room when the first words were spoken, and saw everywhere files of newspapers, old copy and that which was about to be given to the printers. It was very much like an editorial apartment in an American printing office, though in some respects it was different. It was a gloomy apartment, and it seemed to me that the writings of the editor must partake somewhat of the character of the room.

We went into the printing-office, where a hundred hands were setting the "thought-tracks." It seemed as if every one in the building, from editor-in-chief down to the devil, was solemn with the thought of his high and noble avocation. There was a half sadness on every countenance, for the future was full of gloom. I was struck with the fact that the office did not seem to me to be a *French* office. There was a gravity, a solemnity, not often seen in Paris. The usual politeness of a Parisian was there, but no gayety, no recklessness. Anxiety trouble, or fixedness of purpose were written upon almost every countenance. In one corner lay piled up to the ceilings copies of the journal, and I half expected to see a band of the police walk in and seize them. It seemed as if *they* half expected some such thing, but they worked on without saying a word. I became at that moment convinced that a portion of the French people had been wronged by foreigners. There is a large class who are not only intellectual, but they are earnest and grave. They do not wish change for the sake of it. They love liberty and would die for it. Many of this class were murdered in cold blood by Louis Napoleon. Others were sent to Cayenne, to fall a prey to a climate cruel as the guillotine, or were sent into strange lands to beg their bread. These men were the real glory of France, and yet they were forced to leave it.

CHAPTER III.

LAFAYETTE'S TOMB—THE RADICAL—A COUNTRY WALK.

LAFAYETTE'S TOMB.

I am fond of being at perfect liberty to ramble where my fancy may lead. If the sun shine pleasantly this morning, and I would like to hear the birds sing and smell the flowers, I go to some pleasant garden and indulge my mood. Or, if I am sad, I go to the grave of genius, and lean over the tomb of Abelard and Heloise.

When I lived in Paris, I had no regularity in my wanderings, no method in my sight-seeing, following a perhaps wayward fancy, and enjoying myself the better for it.

One beautiful morning I sauntered out from my hotel, with a friend, who was also a stranger in Paris.

"Where shall we go?" he asked.

"To a little cemetery called Picpus, far away from here."

"Will it be worth our while to go so far to see a small cemetery?"

"You shall see when we get there."

We went part of the way by an omnibus, and walked the rest, and when the morning was nearly spent, we stood before No. 15, Rue de Picpus. The place was once a convent of the order of St. Augustine, but is now occupied by the "Women of the Sacred Heart." Within the convent, which we entered, there is a pretty Doric chapel with an Ionic portal. There was an air of privacy about the little chapel which pleased me, and a chasteness in its architecture which could not fail to please any one who loves simple beauty. Within the walls of the court, there is a very small private cemetery, but though private, the porter, if you ask him politely, will let you enter, especially if you tell him you are from America.

"Here is the cemetery which we have come to see," I said to my friend.

"Certainly, it is a very pretty one," he replied; "still I see nothing to justify our coming so far to behold it."

"Wait a little while and you will not say so."

The first group of graves before which we stopped, was that of some victims of the reign of terror—poor slaughtered men and women. The grass was growing pleasantly above them, and all was calm, and sunny, and beautiful around. Perhaps the sun shone as pleasantly when, on the "*Place de la Concorde*," they walked up the steps of the scaffold to die—for *Liberty!* Oh shame! One—two—three—four—there were eight graves we counted, all victims of the reign of terror. For a moment I forgot where I was; the graves were now at my feet, but I saw the poor victims go slowly up to their horrible death. The faces of grinning, scowling devils, male and female, were before me, all clamoring for blood. I could see the tiger-thirst for human flesh in every countenance—the fierce eye—the flushed face—and yet, how still were the winds, how cheerful the sky.

Yet, though every pure-hearted man or woman must detest the horrible cruelties of the great revolution must shudder at the bare mention of the names of the leaders in it, is it not an eternal law of God, that oppression at last produces madness? Have not tyrants this fact always to dream over—*though you* may escape the vengeance of outraged humanity, yet your children, your children's children shall pay the terrible penalty. Louis XVI. was a gentle king; unwise, but never at heart tyrannical; but alas! he answered not merely for his own misdeeds, but for the misdeeds, the tyrannical conduct of centuries of kingcraft. It was an inevitable consequence —and it will ever be so. But I am moralizing.

"You came to see these graves?" remarked my friend. "They are interesting places to ponder and dream over."

"Not to see these, though, did I come," I replied.

We soon came to the graves of nobility. There was the tomb of a Noailles, a Grammont, a Montagu. Plain, all of them, and yet with an air at once chaste and artistic. There was the tomb of Rosambo and Lemoignon amid the tangled grass. All of these names were once noble and great in France, and as I bent over them, I could but call up France in the days of the *ancien régime*, when all these names called forth bows and fawnings from the people. Dead and buried nobility—what is it? The nobility goes—names die with the body.

"You came out to see buried nobility," said my companion.

"Me! Did I ever go out of my way to see even buried *royalty?* Never, unless the ashes had been something more than a mere king. To see the grave of genius or goodness, but not empty, buried names!"

We went on a little farther—to a quiet spot, where the sun shone in warmly, where the grass was mown away short, but where it was green and bright. The song of a plaintive bird just touched our ears—where it was we could not tell, only we heard it. It was a still, beautiful spot, and there was a grave before us—yet how very plain! A pure, white marble, a simple tomb.

Now my companion asked no questions, but I saw that his lips quivered. The name on the simple tomb was that of

"LAFAYETTE."

Here, away from the noise of the city, amid silence chaste and sweet, without a monument, lie the remains of one of the greatest men of France. Not in Pere la Chaise, amid grandeur and fashion, but in a little private cemetery, with a cluster of extinguished nobles on one side, and a band of victims of the reign of terror on the other!

We sat down beside his tomb, grateful to the dust beneath our feet for the noble assistance which it gave to the sinking "Old Thirteen," when the soul of Lafayette animated it. How vividly were the days of our long struggle before us. We saw Bunker Hill alive with battalions, and Charlestown lay in flames. Step by step we ran over the bitter struggle, with so much power on one side, and on the other such an amount of determination, but after all so many dark and adverse circumstances, so little physical power in comparison with the hosts arrayed against us. It was when the heart of the nation drooped with an accumulation of misfortune, that Lafayette came and turned the balance in the scales. And we were grateful to him; not so much for what he really accomplished, as for what he attempted—for the daring spirit, the noble generosity!

Then, too, I thought how Lafayette stood between the king and the people, before and after the reign of terror —thought of his devotion to France—of his stern patri otism, which would neither tremble before a king nor an infuriated rabble. Yet he was obliged to fly for life from Paris—from France. He lay in a felon's dungeon in a foreign land, for lack of devotion to kingcraft, and could not return to France because he loved humanity too well. Was it not hard?

France has never been just to her great men. She welcomes to her bosom her most dangerous citizens, and casts out the true and the noble. She did so when she sent Lafayette away. She did so in refusing Lamartine and accepting Louis Napoleon.

THE RADICAL.

When I first visited Paris, while Louis Napoleon was president of the republic instead of emperor, I became acquainted with a young man from America who had lived seventeen years in Paris. He was thoroughly acquainted with every phase of Parisian life, from the highest to the lowest, and knew the principal political characters of the country. He was a thorough radical, and an enthusiast. He came to Paris for an education, and when he had finished it, he had imbibed the most radical opinions respecting human liberty, and as his native town was New Orleans, and his father a wealthy slaveholder, he concluded to remain in Paris. When I found him, he was living in the Latin quarter, among the students, at a cheap, though very neat hotel. He was refined, modest, and highly educated, and was busy in political writing and speculations. At that time he showed me a complete constitution for a "model republic" in France, and a code of laws fit for Paradise rather than France. The documents exhibited great skill and learning, but the im press of an enthusiast was upon them all. By his conduct or manner, the stranger would never have supposed that my friend was enthusiastic. He never indulged in any flights of indignation at the existing state of things, never was thrown off his guard so as to show by his speech or his manner that he was passionately attached to liberal principles. It was only after I had come to know him well, that I discovered this fact—that he was a great enthusiast, and so deeply attached to the purest principles respecting human freedom and happiness, that he would willingly have died for them. Living in Paris, one of the most dissolute cities of the world, he was pure in his morals, and as rigidly honest as any Puritan in Cromwell's day. But with all his own purity he possessed unbounded charity for others. His friends were among all classes, and were good and bad. One day I saw him walking with one of the most distinguished men of France. A few days after, while he was taking a morning walk, he met a university student with a grisette upon his arm—his mistress. The student wished to leave Paris for the day on business, and asked my friend to accompany his mistress back to their rooms. With the utmost composure and politeness the radical offered his arm, and escorted the frail woman to her apartments.

Of course, this man was carefully watched by the police. He was well known, and the eye of the secret police was constantly upon him. He still clung to his old American passport, for it had repeatedly caused him to be respected when other reasons were insufficient.

I one day wrote a note to a friend in a distant part of the city, and was going to drop it into the post-office when my friend, who was with me, remonstrated. "You can walk to the spot and deliver it yourself," said he, "and you will have saved the two sous postage. I am going that way; let *me* have the postage and I will deliver it."

"I will go with you," I said, at the same time giving him the two sous. He took them without any remonstrance. On the way we met a poor old family, singing and begging in the streets. "They must live," said my friend, "and we will give them our mite in partnership." So he added two sous to those I had given him, and tossed them to the beggars. This was genuine charity, given not for ostentation, but to relieve suffering and administer comfort. I found him at all times entirely true to his principles, and became very much interested in him.

We took a walk together one evening, to hear music in the Luxembourg Gardens. As we approached them, the clock on the old building of the Chamber of Peers struck eight, and at once the band commenced playing some operatic airs of exquisite beauty. Now a gay and enlivening passage was performed, and then a mournful air, or something martial and soul-stirring. The music ceased at nine, and a company of soldiers marched to the drum around the frontiers of the gardens, to notify all who were in it that the gates must soon close.

"What very fine drumming," I said to my companion. "Yes," he replied, "but you should hear a night *rappel*." I heard it often in the days of the June fight. One morning I heard it at three o'clock, calling the soldiers together for battle. You cannot know what a thrill of horror it sent through every avenue of this great city. I got up hastily, and dressed myself and ran into the streets. It was not for me to shrink from the conflict. But the alarm was a false one. Soldiers were in every street, but there was no fighting that day."

A few months before, my friend ventured to publish a pamphlet on the subject of French interference in Italy. He condemned in unequivocal terms the expedition to Italy, and showed how it violated the feelings of the French nation. A few days afterward, he received the following laconic note:

"M. Blank is invited to call on the prefect of the police, at his office, to-morrow, Friday, at eleven oclock."

M. Blank sat down, first, and wrote an able letter to the minister for the interior, for he well knew that the note signified the suppression of the pamphlet, and very likely his ejection from France. He sent the same letter to the American minister, and the next day answered the summons of the prefect. This is the account of the interview which he gave me from a journal he was in the habit of keeping at that time:

"I read the word '*Refugies*' over the door, and it reminded me of the inscription on the gates of hell—'Leave all hope far behind.' Every one knows that the very reason that ghosts are dreaded, is that ghosts were *never seen*. It is the same for policemen—those 'Finders out of Occasions,' as Othello styles them—those 'rough and ready' to choke ideas, as the bud is bit by the venomous worm 'ere it can spread its sweet leaves to the air.' I was about to encounter the assailing eyes of knavery. A gentleman of the administration welcomed me in. 'Sir,' I said, coldly, 'I was invited to meet the *prefect of the police*. I wish to know what is deemed an outrage to the established government of France?'

"The reply, was, 'The procureur-general noticed sev

eral portions of your book; sit down and we will read them!'

"I listened to several extracts, where there were allusions to *princes*, (Louis Napoleon had been formerly a prince, and this was objected to,) and remarked to them that France recognized *no princes*—that what I had written about the expedition to Italy, I had the right, as a publicist, to write. The world had universally repudiated that expedition, and the president had tacitly done the same in his letter to Colonel Ney, and in dismissing the ministers who planned the expedition. The president being quoted as authority, the agent of the executive thought it useless to hold the argument any longer, and backed out. The gentlemen of the police knew nothing of bush-fighting, and might have exclaimed with the muse in Romeo, 'Is this poultice for my aching bones?'"

The upshot of the examination was, that the pamphlet was untouched, and M. Blank remained in Paris.

But he was watched closer than ever. When I left him, he was waiting in daily expectation of a *coup de etat* on the part of Louis Napoleon. I asked him what hopes there were for France. He shook his head sadly—he despaired of success. It might be that Napoleon would be beaten down by the populace, if he attempted to erect a throne, but he had faint hopes of it, for he had got the army almost completely under his influence. Or it was possible that Napoleon might not violate his solemn oaths to support the republic—not for lack of disposition, but fearing the people. I could see, however, that my friend had little faith in the immediate future of "poor France," as he called her, as if she were his mother. He thought the reason why the republic would be overthrown, was from the conduct of those who had been at its head in the early part of its history. The republicans, soon after Louis Philippe's flight, acted, he thought, with great weakness. If strong men had been at the helm, then no such man as Louis Napoleon would have been allowed afterward to take the presidential chair. I think he was more right than wrong. A vigorous and not too radical administration, might have preserved the republic for years—possibly for all time. Louis Napoleon should not have been allowed to enter France, nor any like him, who had proved themselves disturbers of the peace.

About a year after the time I have been describing, while walking down Nassau street, in New York, I very suddenly and unexpectedly met my friend, the radical!

"Aha!" said I, "you have left Paris. Well, you have shown good taste."

"No! no!" he replied, "I did not leave it till Louis Napoleon forced me to choose exile or imprisonment. I had no choice in the matter."

He seemed to feel lost amid the bustle of New York. His dream was over, and at thirty-five he found himself amid the realities of a money-seeking nation. The look upon his face was sad, almost despairing. I certainly never pitied a man more than I did him. Pure, guileless generous—and poor, what could he do in New York?

A WALK INTO THE COUNTRY.

The summer and autumn are the seasons one should spend in Paris, to see it in its full glory. The people of Paris live out of doors, and to see them in the winter, is not to know them thoroughly. The summer weather is unlike that of London. The air is pure, the sky serene, and the whole city is full of gardens and promenades. The little out-of-door theaters reap harvests of money—the tricksters, the conjurors, the street fiddlers, and all sorts of men who get their subsistence by furnishing the people with cheap amusements, are in high spirits, for in these seasons they can drive a fine business. Not so in the winter. Then they are obliged either to wander over the half-deserted *places*, gathering here and there a sou, or shut themselves up in their garret or cellar apartments, and live upon their summer gains. To the stranger who must be economical, Paris in the winter is not to be desired, for fuel is enormously high in that city. A bit of wood is worth so much cash, and a log which in America would be thrown away, would there be worth a little fortune to a poor wood-dealer.

The country around Paris is scarcely worth a visit in the winter or early spring months, but in the summer it is far different. I remember a little walk I took one day past the fortifications. When I came to the walls of the city, I was obliged to pass through a narrow gate. All who enter the city are inspected, for there is a heavy duty upon provisions of nearly all kinds which are brought from the provinces into Paris. The duty upon wines is very heavy. Upon a bottle of cheap wine, which costs in the country but fifteen sous, there is a gate-duty of five sous. This is one reason why the poor people of Paris on *fetê* days, crowd to the country villages near Paris. There they can eat and drink at a much cheaper rate than in town, besides having the advantage of pure air and beautiful scenery. I witnessed an amusing sight at this gate. A man was just entering from the country. He was very large in the abdominal regions, so much so that the gate-keeper's suspicions were aroused, and he asked the large traveler a few leading questions. He protested that e was innocent of any attempt to defraud the revenues of Paris. The gate-keeper reached out his hand as if to examine the unoffending man, and he grew very angry. His face assumed a scarlet hue, and his voice was hoarse with passion, probably from the fact that he was sensitive about his obesity. But the gate-keeper saw in his conduct only increased proof of his guilt, and finally insisted upon laying his hand upon the suspicious part, when with a poorly-concealed smile, but a polite "beg your pardon," he let the man pass on his way. It is probable the gatekeeper was more rigid in his examinations, from the fact that not long before a curious case of deception had occurred at one of the other gates, or rather a case of long-continued deception was exposed. A man who lived in a little village just outside of the walls, became afflicted with the dropsy in the abdominal regions. He then commenced the business of furnishing a certain hotel in Paris with fresh provisions, and for this purpose he visited it twice a day with a large basket on his head or arm. The basket, of course, was always duly examined, and the man passed through. He became well-known to the gatekeeper, and thus weeks and months passed away, until one day the keeper was sure he smelt brandy, and searched the basket more carefully than usual. Nothing was discovered, but the fragrance of the brandy grew stronger, and his suspicions were directed to the man. He was examined, and it was found that his dropsy could easily be cured, for it consisted in wearing something around his body which would contain several gallons, for the man was really small in size, though tall, and he had made it his business to carry in liquors to the city, and evade the taxes. But at last, unfortunately, the portable canteen sprung a leak, and this was the cause which led to the discovery.

At another gate, a woman was detected in carrying quantities of brandy under her petticoats, and only passing for a large woman. I knew of a woman who, in passing the Liverpool custom house, sewed cigars to a great number into her skirt, but was, to her great chagrin, detected, and also to the dismay of her husband, whom she intended to benefit.

Such taxes would not be endured in any American city, but the old world is used to taxation. In the very outskirts of London there are toll-gates in the busiest of streets, but that is not so bad as the local tariff system.

I soon came, in my walk, to the fortifications of Paris. They were constructed by Louis Phillippe, and are magnificent works of defense. There is one peculiar feature of this chain of defense which has excited a great deal of remark. It is quite evident that a part of the fortifications were constructed with a view to defend one's self from enemies *within*, as well as without. Louis Phillippe evidently remembered the past history of Paris, and felt the possibility of a future in which he might like to have the command of Paris with his guns, as well as an enemy outside the wall. But the fortifications and the cannon were of no manner of use to him. So, very possibly, the grand army which Louis Napoleon has raised may be of no use to him, and the little prince, the young king of Algeria, may end his days a wanderer in the United States, as his father was before him. It is to be hoped, if he does, that he will pay his bills.

The fortifications of Paris extend entirely around the city, and are seventeen miles in length. I went to the top of them, but I had not stood there five minutes before the soldiers warned me off. The approach to the city side of the wall is very gradual, by means of a grass-covered bank. While standing upon the summit, a train of cars came whizzing along at a fine rate. I saw for the first time people riding on the tops of cars as on a coach. The train was bound to Versailles, and as the distance is short, and probably the speed attained not great, seats are attached to the tops of the cars, and for a very small sum the poorer classes can ride in them. In fine weather it is said that this kind of riding is very pleasant.

I passed out through the gates beyond the fortifications, and was in the open country—among the trees, the birds and flowers, and the cultivated fields. The contrast between what I saw and the city, was great. Here, all was beautiful nature. There, all that is grand and exquisite in art. The fields around me were green with leaves and plants; the branches of the trees swayed to and fro in the restless breeze; the little peasant huts had a picturesque appearance in the distance, and the laborers at work seemed more healthy than the artisans of Paris. I approached a peasant who was following the plow. I was surprised to find the plow he used to be altogether too heavy for the use to which it was put. Yet I was in sight of Paris, the city of the arts and sciences. Such a plow could not have been found in all New England. I looked at the man, too, and compared him with an American farmer or native workman. He was miserably dressed, and wore shoes which might have been made in the twelfth century. He had no look of intelligence upon his face, but stared at me with a dull and idiotic eye. This was the peasant under the walls of Paris—what must he be in the provincial forests?

Leaving the plowman, I walked on, following a pretty little road, until I came to a large flock of sheep in the care of a shepherd-boy and a dog. While I stood looking at them, the boy started them off across the fields and through the lawns to some other place. All that he did was to follow the sheep, but I certainly never saw a dog so capable and intelligent as that one. He seemed to catch from his master the idea of their destination at once, and kept continually running around the flock, now stirring them into a faster gait, then heading off some wayward fellow who manifested a strong disposition to sheer off to the right or left, and again turning the whole body just where the master wished. It was an amusing sight, and well worth the walk from the city. To be sure, the dog was rather egotistical and ostentatious. He knew his smartness, and was quite willing that bystanders should know it too, for he pawed, and fawned, and barked at a tremendous rate. The flock seemed to know his ways, and while they obeyed his voice, they were not particularly frightened at it.

Leaving the flock and their master, I soon came to a little inn, and sat down to dine. It was not much like the restaurants on the Boulevard, or even like those within the city on retired streets, but I got a very comfortable meal, and for a very small sum of money. I found that the mere mention that I was an American, in all such places as this, insured me polite attention, and I could often notice, instantly, the change of manners after I had informed my entertainers of my country. It is but a slight fact from which to draw an inference, but yet I could not help inferring that the more intelligent of the common people of Paris are yet, notwithstanding the despotism which hovers over France, in their secret hearts longing for the freedom of a just republic.

A young American was a few months since visiting Paris with a much younger brother. The latter went out one day into the country, alone, and seeing that a party of people from Paris were enjoying themselves in the gardens connected with a small public house, he drew near to witness their gayety. They were artisans, but of the most intelligent class. They were neatly dressed, and their faces were bright and intelligent. Whole families were there, down to the little children, and they were enjoying a holiday. Seeing a young man (he was but sixteen years' old) gazing upon them, and judging him to be a stranger, one of the party approached him, and with great politeness asked if he would not come into the garden and drink a glass of wine. The act was a spontaneous one, and arose from good-nature and high spirits. The young American entered, and in the course of a conversation told the company that he was an American. Instantly the scene changed. He was loudly cheered, and one man remarked, with very significant gestures and looks, that "*he came from a republic!*" Nothing would do but that the guest must sit down and accept of food and wine to an alarming extent. He was, in fact, made so much of, that he became somewhat alarmed, for he was young and inexperienced. I may as well finish the story by saying what was the truth, that so many of the party begged the privilege of drinking with him, that he became somewhat giddy and unfit to retrace his steps. He was unused to wine, and the moment the Parisians saw it, they urged him to drink no more, and asking his hotel, they took him carefully and kindly to it in a carriage, after an hour or two had passed away and he had pretty much recovered from his dissipation. Now there can be no doubt that the enthusiastic politeness of the artisans, arose from the fact that he was a republican, and from a great republican country, and such facts which I have repeatedly witnessed, or heard of, assure me that the old republican fire is not extinguished in the hearts of the common people of Paris.

After a frugal dinner at the inn, I sauntered still further into the country, so as, if possible, to get a glimpse of the farm-houses. But one cannot get any fair idea of French agriculture so near Paris. A great deal of the land is used in cultivating vegetables for the Paris markets, and this land is scarcely a specimen of the farms of France, it is more like gardens. I found a few buildings which were occupied by these gardeners, and one or two genuine farmers, and while there was evidently scientific culture bestowed upon the land, the tools were generally clumsy, and altogether too heavy for convenience and dispatch. It struck me as very singular. Paris excels in the manufacturing of light and graceful articles of almost every kind. Certainly, in jewelry, cutlery, and all manner of ornamental articles, it is the first city in the world. How comes it, then, that so near Paris, agricultural implements are so far behind the age? I would by no means have the reader infer that the best of agricultural tools are not manufactured in France. Such is not the fact, as the Paris Exhibition proved, but *who buys them?* Now is it not a significant fact, that within a bow-shot of Paris I found tools in use, which would be laughed at in the free states of America? The true reason for this, is to be found in the condition of the French agricultural laborer. He is ignorant and unambitious. Where the laborer is intelligent, he will have light and excellent tools to work with. This is a universal fact. The slaves of the southern states are in a state of brutal ignorance, and their agricultural implements are heavy and large. Such is the fact with all those men and women who are in a condition somewhat similar. After looking upon the plowman I have before alluded to, I could easily believe what reliable Frenchmen told me—that in the famous (shall I call it *in*famous?) election, very many of the farmers of the interior supposed they were voting for Napoleon the Great, instead of Louis Napoleon!

I passed, in returning to my hotel, one of the finest buildings in Paris—the *Palace d' Orsay.* It was begun in the time of Napoleon, and is a public building.

Palais de Quai D'Orsay.

CHURCH OF NOTRE DAME.

CHAPTER IV.

CHURCHES—NOTRE DAME—L'AUXERROIS—SAINT CHAPELLE —ST. FERDINAND—EXPIATOIRE—MADELEINE, ETC.

NOTRE DAME.

THE churches of Paris are full of gorgeous splendor—how much vital religion they contain, it is not, perhaps, my province to decide. But in beauty of architecture, in the solemnity and grandeur of interior, no city in the world, except Rome, can excel them. The church of the Madeleine is the most imposing of all; indeed, it seemed to me that in all Paris there was no other building so pretentious. But Notre Dame has that mellow quality which beautifies all architecture—hoary age.

I started out one morning to see it, crossing on my way one of the bridges to *Isle la Cité*, and was soon in sight of the two majestic towers of the old cathedral. You can see them, in fact, from all parts of Paris, rising magnificently from the little island city, like beacons for the weary sailor.

The morning was just such an one as Paris delights to furnish in the month of June—fair, clear, and exhilerating—no London fog, mud, or rain, but as soft a sky as ever I saw in America. We stopped a moment before the church, to gaze at the high-reaching columns, and admire the general architecture of the church. Workmen were scattered over different portions of the building and towers, (this was on my first visit to Paris,) engaged in renewing their ancient beauty. My first emotion upon entering, was one of disappointment, for although externally Notre Dame is the finest church in Paris, internally it is gloomy, exceedingly simple, and has an air of faded beauty. Still, the "long-drawn aisles" were very fine. Gazing aloft, the eye ached to watch the beautiful arches meet far above. Then to look away horizontally on either hand through the graceful aisles, filled one with pleasure.

I scarcely know how, but as I was passing a little altar where a priest was saying mass, I unaccountably put my cap upon my head. I was instantly required to take it off. I was reminded of the fact that but a few days before, when entering a Jewish synagogue, upon taking off my hat, I was instantly required to replace it. Such is the difference between the etiquette of a Catholic church and a Jewish synagogue.

I noticed that the threshold of Notre Dame, like that of St. Germain l'Auxerrois, was very much worn away by the feet of the crowds who have crossed it during many centuries. The organ is an excellent one. It is forty-five feet high, thirty-six broad, and has three thousand four hundred and eighty-four pipes. Its power is great, and as the organist touched some of the lower notes, the cathedral walls reverberated with the sound.

The *Porte Rouge* is a splendidly sculptured door-way. Under the arch-way there is a sculpture of Jesus Christ and the Virgin crowned by an angel. Behind it there are bas-reliefs representing the death of the Virgin—Christ surrounded by angels, the Virgin at the feet of Christ in agony, and a woman selling herself to the Devil. The interior of the church abounds with sculpture of every description, and some of it was executed in the twelfth and thirteenth centuries.

There now remains only one of the old peal of bells which used to exist in Notre Dame—but one has escaped the fury of French revolutions. It was hung in the year 1682, and was baptized in the presence of Louis XIV. and Queen Theresa. Its weight is thirty-two thousand pounds—the clapper alone weighing a thousand pounds. A clock in one of the towers is world-renowned for the intricacy and curiosity of its mechanism. The feats it performs every time it strikes the hour and quarter-hour, can hardly be credited by one who has not seen them.

It is supposed that the first foundations of a church on this spot were laid in the year 365, in the reign of Valentian I. It was subsequently several times rebuilt, a portion of the work which was executed in the twelfth and thirteenth centuries still remaining. The other portions were built in 1407, by the duke of Burgundy, and are of a deep red color. The *Porte Rouge* was built under his special superintendence. He assassinated the duke of Orleans, and built this red portal as an expiation for his crime.

In 1831, when the church of St Germain l'Auxerrois was sacked, the mob crowded into Notre Dame and completely destroyed everything within its reach, including, among other things, the coronation robes of Napoleon. The archbishop's palace was next attacked, and in one short hour all its rich stores of ancient and modern literature were thrown into the Seine. The palace itself was so completely ruined, that the government afterward removed every vestige of it. Nothing is more terrible in this world than a mob of maddened people. And though such Vandal acts as these cannot be defended, still it be hooves us to remember, that the conduct of the inhabitants of these palaces was such as to bring down on their heads the just indignation and censure of the people.

Slowly passing through the aisles of the cathedral, I passed again the threshold into the street. The majestic towers and turrets were bright beneath the gaze of the sun, and it seemed to me that I could stand for hours to look at them. It is not so with the Madeleine. Its architectural beauty is great, but it is new—it has no age. Notre Dame has seen centuries, and is full of historical associations, and I could have lingered about it and dreamed over them till the sunlight faded into night.

ST. GERMAIN L'AUXERROIS.

The oldest church in Paris, is called the St. Germain l'Auxerrois. It is one of the quaintest specimens of architecture I ever saw. A church was founded on the spot, many centuries ago, by Childebert. It was of a circular form, and was destroyed by the Normans, in 886. A monastery was established here in 998, and the church at that time was dedicated to St. Germain l'Auxerrois. The ecclesiastics were formed into a college, to which were attached upwards of forty clergymen. It was for many years one of the most celebrated schools in France. In 1744 the college was united to that of Notre Dame, and it was considered to be the college of the royal parish.

This church passed through the terrible scenes of the revolution unscathed, and it would have been perfectly preserved until now, but for a foolish attempt of the royalists to celebrate in it the death of the duke de Berry.

This occurred on the 13th of February, 1831. A great tumult arose, and the interior of the church was entirely destroyed. It was with the greatest difficulty that the furious mob was prevented from tearing it down. On the same day, the palace of the archbishop was also completely devastated. St. Germain l'Auxerrois was now closed, and remained so until 1838. It was then restored, and reöpened for public worship. At one time it was one of the finest interiors in Paris, the royal painters and artists vying with each other in its adornment. It is now, however, only as a third-rate church in its decoration. It is cruciform in shape, with an octagonal termination. At one corner there is a tower which was built in 1649, and some portions of the building were erected in 1400. The western front has a finely sculptured portico, with five low, but rich Gothic arches. The three central ones are higher than the others, and crowned with a parapet. The porch was built in 1431, by Jean Gossel. The other parts of the church were built before the regency of the duke of Bedford. The door-ways are splendidly sculptured, and the church has a rich and ancient appearance.

We entered at one of the little side doors, the friend who was with me remarking,

"See how the feet of centuries have worn away these solid stones."

It was true. A path two feet deep had been worn into the stepping-stone at the entrance. It was a striking exhibition of the power of time.

The interior of this church afforded me one of the most impressive sights I ever witnessed. It had recently been painted in the Byzantine style, and the fresco paintings were as varied and beautiful as the traceries of the frost upon our autumnal woods. You can scarcely conceive the effect it had upon me, just emerged from the eve busy street. The beauty overwhelmed me.

There was a large fresco painting of Christ upon the cross, which particularly arrested my attention. You saw in it every feature of the man, united with the holiness and majesty of the Divine. The face expressed every shade of sweetness and agony; yet it was only a fresco painting. Another represents Christ preaching on the Mount of Olives, with his disciples and the people gathered about him. I was struck with a series of frescoes which were executed to illustrate the most important precepts of Christ. One is that of a warrior, sheathing his sword in the presence of his deadly enemy. It would well grace the walls of a non-resistant, but not those of a French church, which ever reverberate to the music of the drum. The church has generally illustrated that precept of Christ by pictures, not by works. Another of the frescoes represents two brothers embracing each other. Still another, a beautiful young woman giving alms in secret to a poor old blind man. A painting to the right represents Christ issuing the command, "Go ye into all the world, and preach the gospel to every creature." The Magdalen kneels below, in devout admiration, and still lower is the Virgin surrounded by a group of pious women.

On the keystone of one of the vaults, "The Last Supper" is sculptured in solid stone; on another, "The Ordination of the Shepherd." Within the church there are several chapels. The first in the southern aisle contains a magnificent fresco by M. Duval, representing Christ crowning the Virgin. Not far from it there is a fine fresco by Guichard, representing the descent from the cross. The windows upon this side are magnificently decorated with figures of saints and stained glass.

In the center of one transept there is a marble basin for holy water, surmounted by a finely sculptured group of three children supporting a cross. The design is by the donor—the wife of Alphonso de Lamartine, the poet. I noticed in one compartment some admirable traceries in solid oak, and before the high altar an elaborate gilt-bronze lamp—the gift of the wife of Louis Phillippe; but the most brilliant portion of the interior is the fresco painting.

As we walked slowly from chapel to chapel, and transept to transept, I could see men and women—principally the latter—with great apparent devotion kneeling before the altar, or at the confessional. It was not Sunday, yet many people were constantly passing in and out. I might perhaps infer from this fact, that the French possess much religious feeling—but I cannot believe it. Art and literature swallow up religion.

The war-spirit soon eats out vital religion—and revolution and blood sap the morals of any people. The reader will remember that even our revolution rapidly dissipated the good morals of the nation. Never was there a time in the history of New England when vice of every sort made such progress as in the time of the revolution. This is not strange, for war necessarily blunts the religious sensibilities, and opens the door of almost every vice.

We left the interior of the church and stood upon its steps. The Louvre in all its magnificence stood before me. I looked up at the tower of the church, and listened to the very bell which, more than three hundred years ago, gave the signal for the commencement of the massacre of St. Bartholomew. While I stood there it seemed to me that I could go back to the past—to that night of horror, when the Protestants were gathered at the fête of St. Bartholomew. When twelve had struck, in the dead of night, the bell in St. Germain l'Auxerrois gave out the solemn signal, and there ensued a scene of horrible atrocity, such as the world has rarely witnessed, and which will make the names of its perpetrators infamous so long as the world lives.

It was in the house of the dean of St. Germain l'Auxerrois that the beautiful Gabriel d'Estrees lived for awhile and died.

SAINTE CHAPELLE.

The Sainte Chapelle is one of the finest specimens of florid Gothic architecture in the world, and I went with a Frenchman one day to see it. It is impossible to give the reader any adequate idea of its peculiar beauty, but I can briefly sketch it, and at least point out some of its most striking features. It was erected by St. Louis in 1248, and set apart for the reception of relics bought of the emperor of Constantinople. The Chapelle consists of an upper and a lower chapel—the upper communicating with the old palace of the ancient kings of France. It was formerly appropriated to the king and court. The lower chapel opens into the lower courts of the palace, and was appropriated to the use of the common people in and around the palace. The interior has of late undergone extensive repairs, and it is now thoroughly restored.

The entrance is unpleasant, for it is very narrow—so much so that a good view of the front cannot be had. It has a portico of three Gothic arches with intersecting buttresses, and in connection with lateral buttresses there are two spiral towers with spiral stair-cases. Between the towers there is a splendid circular window, which was constructed by Charles VIII. The spires of the church are octagonal, and are adorned with mouldings and traceries, and also at about half-height with a crown of thorns. The different sides of the Chapelle are in the same style—with buttresses between the windows, gables surmounting these, and a fine open parapet crowning all. The roof is sloping, and the height is over a hundred feet. The spire measures, from the vaulting, seventy feet. We entered by a stair-case the upper chapel, and an exquisite view presented itself. A single apartment, a half-circular chair, with fine, large windows, detached columns with bases and capitals, and fine groining—these all strike the eye of the visitor as he crosses the threshold. The whole is gorgeously painted and interspersed with *fleur de lis.* In the nave there is a carved wooden stair-case of the thirteenth century. The windows are filled with stained glass of 1248, which has escaped destruction during two great revolutions.

Near the altar there is a side chapel, to which access is had from below. Here Louis XI. used to come, amid the choicest relics, and say his prayers. Some of the relics are still preserved, and consist of a crown of thorns, a piece of the cross upon which Christ was crucified, and many antique gems. The Chapelle and the relics cost Louis two millions eight hundred thousand francs—the relics alone costing an enormous amount.

There was a richly endowed chapter in connection with the Chapelle and what is a little singular, the head of it became renowned for his litigous disposition. The poet

Boileau, in *Lutrin*, satirized this character—and was, after death, buried in the lower chapel.

At the time of the great revolution, this ancient and beautiful building escaped destruction by its conversion by the government into courts of justice. The internal decorations were, however, many of them destroyed. The church, as it exists now, in a state of complete restoration, is one of the finest church interiors in Paris, and the best specimen of its peculiar kind of architecture in the world.

My friend was a little surprised at the enthusiasm I manifested. *He* seemed to look as coolly upon the exquisite architectural beauty, and to contemplate the age of the building as quietly, as a farmer would survey his promising wheat-field. I reminded him that I came from a land where such things do not abound, and where one cannot gratify the desire to look upon that which is not only ancient, but around which cluster the choicest historical associations.

CHAPELLE EXPIATOIRE.

While wandering one day though the Rue d'Anjou St. Honoré, I came unexpectedly upon one of the most beautiful chapels my eyes ever beheld—the *Chapelle Ex piatore.* It was originally a burial-ground in connection with the Madeleine church, but was afterward set apart to commemorate the sad fate of the elder Bourbons. When Louis XVI. and his queen were executed, in 1793, they were obscurely buried on this spot. A friend, M. Descloseaux, at once cared for their remains, else they would have been lost amid other victims of the bloody revolution. It is a singular fact, that Danton, Herbert, and

Robespierre were also buried in this same place, together with the Swiss Guard.

An early entry in the parish records of the Madeleine, still shows to any one who has the curiosity to see, the plainness with which the queen was buried. It is as follows: "*Paid seven francs for a coffin for the Widow Capet.*"

M. Descloseaux watched carefully over the graves of the king and queen, purchased the place containing their bodies, and converted it into an orchard, with the view of shielding them from the fury of the populace. His plan was successful, and it is said that he sent every year a beautiful bouquet of flowers to the duchess d'Angoulême, which were gathered from the ground beneath which her royal parents were sleeping.

The restoration came, and the orchard was purchased from M. Descloseaux. The bodies were transferred to St. Denis, with great pomp. The earth which had surrounded the coffins was preserved, as also were all remains of the Swiss Guards, and buried on the spot. Over it an expiatory chapel was built, with buildings adjoining, the whole forming a very beautiful structure. An inscription on the front informs the gazer of the principal facts I have enumerated. The adjoining garden is filled with cypresses.

The interior of the chapel is simple, but gives a pleasant impression. It contains two statues, one of Louis XVI., and the other of Marie Antoinette. Each is supported by an angel, and on the pedestal of the king his will is inscribed in letters of gold, upon a black marble slab. On the pedestal of the queen's statue are extracts, executed in a like manner, from her last letter to Mme. Elizabeth.

There are several niches in the chapel which contain

very fine candelebra, and on a bas-relief the funeral procession to St. Denis is represented.

I was struck while here (as indeed I was in many other places) with the fact, that the whole past history of Paris and France is written in her chapels and churches. The stranger cannot, if he would, shut out the fact from his sight. It glares in upon him from every street. The revolutions of France have imprinted themselves upon Paris in ineffaceable characters.

As I stood in this chapel, the sad history of Marie Antoinette came into my thoughts, and she stood before me as she stood before the crowd on the day of her execution. Her downfall, the wretched neglect with which her poor body was treated, and the obscure burial, were all before me. Only "seven francs," for the coffin of "Widow Capet!" What a contrast to the pomp and ceremony of her second burial, aye what a contrast to her life!

I had seen enough for that day, and set out sadly on my way back to my apartments. The gayety in the streets, the bright and balmy air, could not take the hue of melancholy from my thoughts. For always to me the history of Marie Antoinette has been one of the most sorrowful I ever read. I have few sympathies for kings, and much less for kingly tyrants, but I could never withhold them from her, queen though she was. And I never wish to become so fierce a democrat that I can contemplate such sorrows as were hers, such a terrible downfall as she experienced, with a heartless composure.

Eglise de la Madeleine.

THE MADELEINE.

The Madeleine looks little like a church to the stranger, but more like a magnificent Grecian temple. Its impression upon me was by no means a pleasant one, for the style of its architecture is not sufficiently solemn to suit my ideas of a place where God is publicly worshiped. It is, however, one of the finest specimens of modern architecture in the world, and is so widely known that I can hardly pass it over without a slight sketch of it.

An edifice was erected on the spot where the Madeleine stands, in 1659, by Mademoiselle d'Orleans. That building was soon found to be too small for the accommodation of the people in its neighborhood, and in 1764, the present building was commenced by the architect of the duke of Orleans. The revolution put an end for a time to the work upon the church, but Napoleon, after his Prussian campaign, determined to dedicate the Madeleine as a Temple of Glory, "to commemorate the achievements of the French arms, and to have on its columns engraved the names of all those who had died fighting their country's battles." The necessary funds were given, and architects were set at work immediately upon it. But Napoeon's plans were frustrated, and in 1815 Louis XVIII. restored the building to its original destination, and ordered that monuments should be erected in it to Louis XVI., Marie Antoinette, Louis XVII., and Mme. Elizabeth. The revolution of 1830, however, interrupted this work, and it was not till the reign of Louis Phillippe, that it was completed. The entire cost of the Madeleine was two millions six hundred and fifteen thousand and eight hundred dollars. It stands on a raised platform, three hundred and twenty-eight feet long and one hundred and thirty-eight broad, and has at each end an approach consisting of twenty-eight steps, the entire length of the facade. The architecture is Grecian, a colonnade of fifty-two Corinthian columns entirely surrounding the building, giving to it a grandeur of appearance to which few structures in Europe attain. Between the columns there are niches, and a row of colossal statues stand in them. They represent St. Bernard, St. Raphael, and a score of others. The colonnade is surmounted by a beautiful piazza, and a cornice adorned with lion's heads and palm leaves.

The pediment of the southern end contains a large alto-relievo by Lemaire. It is one hundred and twenty-six feet long and twenty-four feet high. In the center is a figure of Christ; the Magdalene is beneath in a suppliant attitude; while HE is pardoning her sins. On the right hand the angel of Pity gazes down upon the poor woman, with a look of deep satisfaction. On the other hand is the figure of Innocence, surrounded by the angels, Faith,

Hope, and Charity. In the angle of the pediment is the figure of an angel greeting the new-born spirit, and raising his hand, points to the place prepared for him in heaven.

On the left of the pediment the angel of Vengeance is repelling the Vices. Hatred is there with swollen features; Unchastity, with disheveled hair and negligent dress, clings to her guilty paramour; Hypocrisy, with the face of a young woman, a mask raised to her forehead, looks down upon the spectator; and Avarice is represented as an old man clinging to his treasures.

The pediment is filled completely by the figure of a demon, which is forcing a damned soul into the abyss of woe. This is the largest sculptured pediment in the world, and occupied more than two years in its execution. The figure of Christ is eighteen feet in length, which will give the reader an idea of the size of the sculpture.

The doors of the Madeleine are worthy of particular notice. They are of bronze, measuring more than thirty feet by sixteen. They are divided into compartments each of which illustrates one of the Ten Commandments. In the first, Moses commands the tables to be obeyed; in the second, the blasphemer is struck; in the third, God reposes after the creation; in the fourth, Joshua punishes the theft of Acham, after the taking of Jericho, etc. etc. The doors were cast in France, and are only surpassed in size by the doors of St. Peter's.

On entering the Madeleine, the magnificent organ meets the eye of the visitor. On the right, there is a chapel for marriages, with a sculptural group upon it, representing the marriage of the Virgin. On the left, there is a baptismal font, with a sculptured group, representing Christ and St. John at the waters of the Jordan. There are twelve confessionals along the chapels, which, together with the pulpit, are carved out of oak. The walls of the church are lined with the finest marbles, and each chapel contains a statue of the patron saints. The architecture of the interior it is useless for me to attempt to sketch, it is in such a profusely ornamented style. Fine paintings adorn the different chapels. One represents Christ preaching, and the conversion of Mary Magdalene; another the Crucifixion; still another, the supper at Bethany, with the Magdalene at the feet of her Lord. Over the altar there is a very fine painting by Ziegler, which intends to illustrate, by the representation of persons, the events which, in the world's history, have added most to propagate the christian religion, and to exhibit its power over men.

The Magdalene, in a penitent attitude, stands near Christ, while three angels support the cloud upon which she kneels, and a scroll, upon which is written, "*She loved much.*" The Savior holds in his right hand the symbol of redemption, and is surrounded by the apostles. On his left, the history of the early church is illustrated. St. Augustine, the Emperor Constantine, and other personages, are painted. Then follow the Crusades, with St. Bernard and Peter the Hermit, with a group of noblemen following, filled with holy enthusiasm.

Near the Magdalene there is a group of men who figured in early French history—the Constable Montmorenci, Godefroy de Bouillon, and Robert of Normandy. The struggles of the Greeks to throw off Mussulman rule, are represented by a young Grecian warrior, with his companions in arms.

On the left of the Savior, some of the early martyrs are painted—St. Catherine and St. Cecelia. The Wandering Jew's ghostly form is upon the canvas, and, to come down to a later day, Joan of Arc, Raphael, Michael Angelo, and Dante each occupies a place in the mammoth picture.

The choir of the Madeleine forms a half-circle, and is very richly ornamented. The great altar is splendidly sculptured. The principal group represents the Magdalene in a rapturous posture, borne to heaven on the wings of angels. A tunic is wrapped around her body, and the long hair with which she wiped her Savior's feet. This group of sculpture alone cost one hundred and fifty thousand francs.

I have thus given the reader a sketch of the most gorgeous church in Paris, that he may get an idea of the style of religion which obtains at present there. It is like this church. It is pretentious, imposing, in bad taste, without simplicity and a real sanctity. I was disgusted with the Madeleine from the moment I knew it to be a church. At first I saw it only as a fine building—an imitation of the Parthenon—and I was struck with admiration. But when I was told that it was a temple for the worship of God, I was shocked, and still more so when I entered it. The interior, as a collection of fine paintings and statues, as a specimen of gorgeous Gothic architecture, is one of the best in the world; but I would as soon think of attending public worship amid the nakedness of the Louvre, as in the Madeleine. Had Napoleon's idea been carried out, and this modern Parthenon been dedicated to Mars, it would adorn Paris, and add much to the pleasure of the stranger; but as it is now, it only serves to illustrate one of the weak points in the French character.

The genuine Parisian is so fond of appearance, that he cares little for the substance. The churches of Paris, therefore, abound with all that can impress the eye, however repugnant to a refined taste. For I dare to hold, that the French love not the true refinement in matters of religion. Having little vital piety, it is impossible for them to judge of church architecture. Solemn old St. Paul's in London, will always linger in my memory as a fit temple of the living God. Its impressive grandeur contrasts strongly with the rich magnificence of the Madeleine. The latter inspires only admiration, as the figure of a Greek warrior, but St. Paul's inspires awe; and that is just the difference between them.

CHAPEL OF ST. FERDINAND.

The interior of this chapel is one of the most beautiful in Paris. It was the scene of the death of the duke of Orleans in 1842. He left Paris in the forenoon of the 13th of July, in an open carriage, with but one postillion, intending to call upon the royal family at Neuilly, and proceed to the camp at St. Omer. As he approached Porte Maillot, the horses became frightened. The driver began to lose his control of the horses.

"Are you master of your horses?" asked the duke.

"Sir, I guide them," was the reply.

"I am afraid you cannot hold them," again cried the duke.

"I cannot, sir," was the reply.

The duke then endeavored to get out of the carriage, but his feet became entangled in his cloak, and he was thrown with great force to the ground, his head striking first. It was dreadfully fractured, and he was carried into the house of a grocer near at hand, where he expired at four o'clock the same day, entirely unconscious. The royal family were with him when he died. The house with the adjacent property was bought, and two distinguished architects were commanded to erect a commemorative chapel on the place. In July, 1843, it was consecrated by the archbishop, in the presence of the royal family.

The building is fifty feet long, twenty in height, is built in the Lombard-Gothic style, and resembles an ancient mausoleum.

Opposite the entrance there stands an altar to the Virgin, on the very spot where the duke breathed his last, and over it there is a strikingly beautiful statue of the Virgin and child. Beyond, there is a Descent from the Cross in marble. On the left, is another altar dedicated to St. Ferdinand, and on the right a marble group, which represents the duke on his death-bed. An angel kneels at his head, as if imploring the Divine Mercy upon the sufferer. It is a fine figure, and is doubly interesting from the fact that the Princess Marie, sister of the duke, with her own hands wrought it, long before he was still in death. Beneath this marble group there is a bas-relief, representing France leaning over, and near, the French flag drooping at her feet. There are four circular windows of stained glass, with St. Raphæl, Hope, Faith, and Charity, upon them. There are fourteen pointed windows, stained with the patron saints of the royal family. Behind the altar the very room is preserved in which the duke died—the sacristy of the chapel now. The oaken presses, chairs, and prayer-desk are all clothed in black, giving an air of gloom to the whole apartment. Opposite the entrance there is a large painting by Jacquard, representing the death of the duke. He is lying upon a couch with his head supported by physicians; his father is opposite, apparently stupefied by his deep emotions. On the left is a group, consisting of the queen and Princess Clementine, the Dukes Aumale, and Montpensier, Marshals Soult, Gerard, and the curé of Méry. The picture is a touching one. There is a small apartment detached from the chapel, which was fitted up for the accommodation of the royal family—the family now exiled from the land. In another room there is a clock with a black marble case, on which France is represented as mourning for the death of the duke. The hands of the clock mark ten minutes to twelve, the exact moment when the prince fell; and in another apartment there is a clock with the pointers at ten minutes past four, the moment when he died.

The interior of this chapel impressed me as the saddest I ever was in. Everything in it was in perfect keeping with the sentiment of complete melancholy, though it was rather too luxurious to express deep grief. Sorrow which is poignant, is not expressed in so sensuous a manner. But the chapel is unique; there is nothing else like it in the world, and that is quite a recommendation.

ST. VINCENT DE PAULE.

In my enumeration of the splendid churches of Paris, it would never do to omit that of St. Vincent de Paule. It is in the Rue Lafayette, and is now a Protestant church.

The approaches to the building are fine, and the structure forms a parallelogram of two hundred and forty-three feet by one hundred and eighty. At the southern end, there are two large towers with Corinthian pilasters. The church stands upon the brow of a hill, and presents a striking appearance from the streets Lafayette or Hauteville.

The interior of this church is profusely decorated, and is, in fact, so richly ornamented as to detract from its beauty. Over the portal, there is a stained window representing St. Paule surrounded by the sisters of charity. The choir is semi-circular, and has a fine skylight. A richly sculptured arch, over sixty feet in height, gives access to it. The altar-piece is a crucifix on wood. Behind it is a stained window, representing the Virgin and the Savior. The chapels have also beautifully stained windows. There are no oil-paintings in St. Vincent de Paule, but in other respects it is as faulty as the Madeleine. It may be the result of early education, but I sickened of this excess of ornament. It was too forced—too unnatural. If I had never entered the church I should have received a good impression, for its exterior is everything of which the Ionic order is capable, and its situation is the finest of any church in Paris.

I will simply allude to a few of the other churches in Paris. The *Notre Dame de Lorette*, is a very beautiful church in the street *Fountain St. George.* It is built in the renaissance style, and the sculptures of the interior are of the highest order. The gorgeous decorations of the church are unsurpassed. The interior is one blaze of splendor, and the feelings inspired by a contemplation of it, are not the ones appropriate for a place of worship. The choir of the church is fitted up with stalls, a gilt balustrade separating it from the rest of the nave. The walls are adorned with rich marbles. The altar is executed in the highest style of magnificence. Behind it is a piece entitled "The Crowning of the Virgin," wrought on a background of pure gold. The Parisians boast a great deal of this church, as a gem of the renaissance style, and with reason, when it is regarded simply as a work of art, but the less they boast of it as *a church*, the better. The cost was one million eight hundred thousand francs.

St. Roch, in the *Rue St. Honoré*, was built under the patronage of Louis XIV. and Anne of Austria, in 1653. The renowned financier, Law, gave one hundred thousand livres toward its completion. The steps are high, and from them crowds of people during the revolution saw the executions which took place but a short distance away. A mob once filled the steps, and were cleared away by Napoleon's cannon. The duke of Orleans, and Corneille, the poet, lie buried in it, together with other distinguished persons. St. Roch is not beautiful in its architectural decorations, but is, nevertheless, the richest church in Paris.

St. Eustache is the largest church, except Notre Dame, in Paris, and is very old. The style is a mixed Gothic.

The *St. Paul et St. Louis*, is a church built in the Italian style, and is a fine edifice.

All the churches of Paris are open every day of the week, from early in the morning till five or six o'clock. They have bare pews or slips, and no seats. There are a plenty of chairs which may be had on Sundays and festival days, for two cents each, of an old woman who attends them. This custom is a singular one to the American, accustomed as he is to well-cushioned, and even luxurious pews. The pulpits, too, are nothing but upright boxes, with a spiral staircase leading to them—not like our broad platforms, with rich sofas and tables in front.

Church of St. Eustache.

CHAPTER V.

LAMARTINE—HORACE VERNET—GIRARDIN—HUGO—JANIN

LAMARTINE.

LAMARTINE is a poet, a historian, and a statesman. He has not been successful in the last-mentioned capacity, but take his qualities together, he is, perhaps, the most distinguished of living French authors.

Alphonse de Lamartine was born on the 21st of Octo

ber, 1791, at Mecon. His father was captain in a regiment of cavalry. Refusing to join with the terrorists in 1794, he fled from Paris into the country with his wife and two children. But he did not escape the spies of his enemies, who arrested and put him at once into a dungeon. Some months after, the terrorists having lost power, he was released. Resolving to provide for the future peace of his family, he purchased the chateau of Milly, a spot in the open, and nearly wild country. Lamartine gives us sketches of his life here. His mother was a good, pious soul, and taught him out of the old family bible lessons from the sacred scriptures. She often made visits to the poor, and Alphonse accompanied her on these benevolent errands, and thus very early in life learned to be gentle and good. He left the grounds of Milly at eight years of age, to enter the school of Belley, under the care of the Jesuits.

He took the prizes with ease, and his teachers discovering that he had a talent for poetry, encouraged it. His parents took counsel as to what should be done with their son. The father wished to make a soldier of him, but the mother was opposed to this plan—she did not care to make a human butcher of her boy. He paused some time at Lyons, on his return from school, and afterward he traveled over Italy. He here met a young man who was an excellent singer, and became quite intimate with him, so much so, that he often slept upon his shoulder. When the two friends had arrived at Rome, Lamartine was called down to the breakfast-room one morning, to behold—*not* his male companion, but a young woman of beauty, who greeted him familiarly. It was his friend who had been traveling in male costume, and who now said blushingly, "Dress does not change the heart."

Lamartine went to Naples and his purse ran low, when he chanced to meet an old classmate who had plenty of money, and together the young men enjoyed their good fortune. At Naples, Graziella, the daughter of a poor fisherman, fell in love with the poet. The story of this girl he tells very touchingly. When he returned home he was welcomed very warmly. The family had removed to Mecon. His mother grew pale and trembling, to see how long absence and agony of heart had changed her son. She told him that their fortune had been considerably affected by his travels and imprudences, and she spoke not by way of reproach, for said she, "You know that if I could change my tears into gold, I would gladly give them all into your hands."

He wished to go to Paris, and his father gave him, for his maintenance, the moderate sum of twelve hundred francs a year. The mother pitied her son, and going to her room, she took her last jewel and put it into his hands, saying, "Go and seek glory!" He took a plenty of recommendations with him, but was resolved to accept nothing from the emperor. When a young man he had dreamed of a republic, but now, after coming to Paris, he became a Bonapartist. He entered the most aristocratic circles, and changed again to a legitimist. He now made a second voyage to Italy, following the inclinations of his dreamy nature. During his stay there, he composed the first volume of his *Meditations*, which afterward won him so much fame.

He was on the borders of the gulf of Naples, when he heard of the establishment of the Bourbon dynasty, and he hastened home and solicited a place in the army, to the great joy of his father. During the Hundred Days he threw aside the sword, and would not take it again when Louis XVIII. regained the throne.

Lamartine now loved a young woman devotedly, but she died, to his excessive grief. He was severely ill from this cause, and it wrought a great change in his character. When recovered from his illness, he destroyed his profane poetry, and kept only that which bore the impress of faith and religion. He published his first volume of *Meditations* in 1820. He sought in vain two years for a publisher, until at last a man by the name of Nicoll, as a personal favor, issued the volume. It made his fortune. France welcomed the new poet as a redeemer, who had dispelled the materialism of Voltaire. He became an *attache* of the ambassador in Tuscany, and there met a young English woman, who was in love with him before she saw him, from reading his *Meditations*. This woman he shortly married. She brought him beauty, goodness, and a large fortune.

In 1823 the second volume of *Meditations* appeared, and had the same success as the first. An uncle died at this time, leaving him a fortune, and he was now independent of the world. He lived alternately in London and in Paris, occasionally accepting the post of secretary to a foreign ambassador, and finally becoming charg d'affaires at an Italian court. Like almost all the distinguished authors of France, Lamartine fought his duel. He had written something disparaging to modern Italy, and one Colonel Pepe, an Italian, challenged him to fight a duel. He accepted the challenge and was wounded. For six months he hung between life and death. All Florence condemned with severity the brutal colonel, who had taken offense at one of the poet's verses, and they came to inquire for his health every hour of the day, as if he had been a monarch. When he left Florence, great was their sorrow. In the midst of his diplomatic labors he continued to write poetry, and on his return to Paris in the month of May, 1829, he published "*Harmonies Poetiques et Reliegieuses*," and this book created for him such a reputation, and gave him so much honor, that in 1830 he was elected a member of the Academy.

The government about this time was resolved upon sending a minister plenipotentiary to Greece, and Lamartine was chosen as the man; but at this juncture the revolution broke out, and the project fell to the ground. The poet was discouraged, and went to live in the country, on an estate bequeathed to him by one of his uncles. He soon became tired of his quiet life, and took ship at Marseilles, with his wife and his daughter Julia, for the Orient. The vessel was his own, and he sailed at pleasure. France lost for a time her brilliant son, but gained therefor a beautiful book—*Le Voyage en Orient.* It achieved a great success, and if he would have been content with literary renown, he now could have wished for nothing more to add to his happiness. While he was absent in the East, he kept an eye upon the politics of home.

His daughter Julia was taken very ill at Beyrout, and died. She was brought back to Marseilles in her coffin. This was a terrible blow to the poet, who possessed as soft a heart as ever throbbed in the breast of woman.

During his absence, the electors of Dunkirk decided to offer Lamartine a seat in the Chamber of Deputies, and he was elected. Well had it been for the poet if he had rested satisfied with his literature, but he entered the field of politics to become distinguished, but to win no laurels. He was unsuccessful, at first, in the Chamber. He became a radical, and that party flattered him. They were poor—he was rich and generous. He gave freely for his party, and found himself almost penniless. He gave to all who needed, so long as he had anything to give. At this time a man wrote to him—"I die of hunger." The poet sent five hundred francs, and begged pardon for not sending more, adding—"You have all my heart."

At this time the *History of the Girondins* appeared, and had a remarkable success. Lamartine was severely blamed by many for writing it, but none disputed the wonderful literary merit of the work. The next revolution came—and Louis Phillippe fled from France. The people flocked around Lamartine. They had been charmed by his grand words for humanity; they were now fascinated by his commanding mien and noble countenance. They thought because he sang sweetly, wrote nobly, that he was a statesman. They mistook. The author had no talents for statesmanship, and he fell. He was too ideal—not sufficiently practical; and he could not hold the position which the populace had given him. For a short time his ambition—never an impure one—was gratified, for he saw France turn toward him as a deliverer; but he has ever since had the bitter reflection that he was unequal to the occasion, and that he had acted wisely never to have invaded the domain of politics.

The history of Lamartine during the revolution of 1848 is everywhere known, and we need not repeat it. He soon gave up politics forever. Since that time he has attended only to literature. Recently, he ventured into speculations, and lost his fortune. I had the good luck to meet him last June, in the office of the editor of *L'Illustration*, in the Rue Richelieu. He was in good health, and I was much struck with his general appearance. He looks to be what he has always been—one of nature's noblemen. His hair is almost white, but his figure is erect and noble. He is tall and dignified, and his manners are pleasing. Lamartine has struggled hard to save from the hands of his creditors his estate of Saint Point, where the bones of his ancestors lie. Every autumn he repairs thither with Madame Lamartine, and spends a few months in the golden quiet of the country. His wife is the angel of his household, and has proved a treasure far above earthly riches. Both husband and wife are exceedingly generous. A friend of theirs, who was very intimate with the family, was so angered at their liberality, that he one morning entered the house, demanding all the keys, and declaring that he would for a time take charge of their expenses. They willingly acceded to his demand. He locked up everything valuable, and left the house. Soon a sister of charity came, and sought alms for the poor. Madame Lamartine tried the desk for money—it was locked. She called the valet and had it broken open, and gave the sister eight hundred francs. Lamartine smiled, and kissed her for the generous act. The friend returned and found that there was not money enough left for dinner!

Lamartine possesses a noble heart, a conscience, and is a christian. He is a bright example, but alas! a rare one, among the authors of France.

HORACE VERNET.

Horace Vernet, the great modern painter of France, was born in the Louvre on the 30th of June, 1789. The kings of France were in the habit of giving to distinguished artists a domicile in the Louvre, and the father of Horace Vernet, at the time of his birth, had apartments in the palace. He is descended from a dynasty of artists.

Antoine Vernet, the great-grandfather of Horace, lived in the time of Mademoiselle de L'Enclos, a very celebrated courtesan, and it is said by some that he was the author of the portrait of her which exists at this day, but it is proved that he never left Argnon, where he lived as an artist. The grandfather of the subject of this sketch --Claude-Joseph Vernet—studied in Rome, and became a distinguished marine painter under the reign of Louis XV., who commissioned him to paint a series of pictures. Carle Vernet, the father of Horace Vernet, was also an artist. When quite young, he fell violently in love with the daughter of an opulent furnisher. The marriage was impossible, and his friends, to wean him from his love, sent him to Italy, where he studied the art of painting, and took a high prize—but he could not forget the woman he had loved. In his grief he resolved to give himself up to a monastic life, and his letters from Italy apprised his friends of that fact. His father hastened to Italy and brought him back to France, where he at once acquired distinction as a painter, and was elected a member of the Academy of Painting. He painted several grand battle-scenes under the empire, and in 1789 became the father of the Horace Vernet, so justly distinguished in modern times.

Horace was taught the art of his father, and he learned to draw at the same time that he learned to read. In 1793 the family of artists experienced many dangers, and on the 18th of August, while his father and Horace were crossing the court of the Tuileries palace, Horace was shot through the hat, while a ball pierced the clothes of the father. Carle Vernet was about to hasten from France when new terrors detained him. His sister had married M. Chalgrin, an architect, who adhered to the fortunes of the court of Provence. For this, the mob had revenge upon his beautiful wife, who was thrown into the Abbaye prison. Carle Vernet hastened to his brother artist, David, who was in favor with the revolutionists.

and who could easily save his sister's life. He besought David to save his sister, but he coolly replied:

"She is an aristocrat, and I will not trouble myself about her." She perished, and the reason was, that in early life she had refused the matrimonial offers of the painter.

The youthful Horace was reckoned very beautiful by all his friends, and especially by his father. He was a model, in fact, and as he grew up, he showed that he had inherited the artist-genius of his father, and added to it a wit peculiarly his own. His sallies were often exceedingly amusing to the people in whose company he chiefly spent his time. He entered college, and as soon as he had quitted it he was already distinguished as an artist. Instead of going back to ancient times, he painted his own age. He was enthusiastic in all his efforts, and catching the spirit of the times, grew rapidly popular. He did not live in the past, but in the living present, and endeavored to glorify the men, deeds, and places of to-day.

The figure of Vernet was small, his face was fine-looking, his hand white, and his foot very small. He went to masked balls and arrayed himself as a woman, and was constantly importuned by suitors. On one occasion a marshal of France was so pressing in his suit, that he put himself under the care of his wife, who took the supposed lady home with her in the family carriage!

From 1811 to 1815 Vernet appeared at court and was quite popular. He painted portraits of the different members of the royal family. He was so celebrated for his drawings, that the editors disputed for them, and paid him the highest prices. In 1814 he was decorated with the cross of the Legion of Honor. At the restoration, he for a time was under a cloud. He was not idle, but such were his subjects that he was shut out of the Louvre. He, however, executed many paintings, which subsequently became celebrated. Disgusted with the treatment he received, he journeyed with his father into Italy.

The Louvre continued shut against Vernet's pictures, but the peers took up his cause with great unanimity and enthusiasm. A list of his best pictures was published and warmly eulogized, and as they could be seen at his studio, the crowd of artists and critics, and others, wended their way thither. The painter was recompensed. In the midst of this crowd, and the confusion necessarily consequent upon their visit, Horace Vernet went on quietly in his work, in their presence, and executed that series of grand paintings, which in after years brought him so wide a renown. The duke of Orleans was his warm friend. He bought many pictures of him, and ordered himself painted in every style. Charles X. grew jealous, and concluded it wise to withdraw his persecution of the artist. He ordered a portrait of himself, and the Louvre was open to him.

He now wrought a revolution in the art of painting in Paris, and established a new school. It was his desire to triumph over David, and he boasted that he would do so. The public pronounced him the first painter of the age. Some of his best pictures at this time were painted at Rome. Upon his return he found his old friend king, under the title of Louis Philippe. He was, of course, a favorite at court. The king gave him the use of a studio at Versailles, of a magnificent description, in which he wrought at great national pictures. He was an indefatigable worker. He never hesitated to make the longest journey to study the scene of his pictures. He traveled up and down the Mediterranean, visited Arabia, Africa, and other distant spots, lived in tents, put up with privation and suffering, that he might paint from nature. His memory was so excellent that having once looked upon a spot, nothing was afterward forgotten; every characteristic of the place was sure to reäppear upon the canvas. The least detail of position or gesture, he remembered for years with ease. Indeed, his faculty for daguerreotyping such things upon his mind, was wonderful. He met his friend, the marquis de Pastorel, one day, who said:

"How are you, Horace; where have you kept yourself for these two years? I have not met you for years."

"You are mistaken," replied the artist; "I met you six months since in the garden of the Tuileries."

"You are dreaming," said the marquis.

"No," said Vernet, "a lady was with you—wait a moment and I will sketch her face."

He drew a few hasty lines upon a bit of paper, and lo! the marquis beheld the face of an intimate lady friend of his, and at the same instant remembered that he had escorted her across the Tuileries gardens six months before.

"It is well for you that you live *now*," said the marquis, "for two centuries earlier they would have burned you for a sorcerer."

Horace Vernet has been a great student of the scriptures, and he maintains that in painting historical scenes from the bible, the costumes should be such as the Arabians use at this time, and in his scripture paintings he has followed out this plan.

In 1834 and 1835 he was principally on the coast of Africa, engaged in painting. But he returned to his studio at Versailles, and in 1836 produced several grand battle-pictures. The king desired that he should fill an entire gallery with his pictures at Versailles, and Vernet went at his giant work. He occupied six years, and the gallery was called *la Galerie de Constentine.* The king came into his studio one day, and offered to make Vernet a peer. The painter declined the honor, saying "the *bourgeois* rise—the nobles fall—leave me with the arts."

He was one day painting *the Siege of Valenciennes* for the king, when the latter requested that the painter would represent Louis XIV. as prominent in the siege. Vernet consulted history, and found that during the siege the king was three leagues away with one of his mistresses. He therefore utterly refused to lie upon canvas. The king was very angry, and several persons were sent to persuade Vernet to consent, *for pay*, to make the concession. He however remained firm, and picking up his effects and selling his pictures, started for St. Petersburgh, where he was received with open arms by Nicholas. While at the Russian court, Vernet spoke freely his sentiments, and condemned the taking of Poland. "Bah!" said the Czar, "you look from a French point of view—I from the Russian. I dare say, now, you would refuse to paint me *the taking of Warsaw.*"

"No, sire," replied the painter, sublimely; "every day we represent Christ upon the cross!"

Louis Philippe sent by his ambassador for Vernet to return to Paris. "You may paint the Siege of Valenciennes without any Louis XIV. in it, if you please," he said. The painter was received warmly, and the old quarrel was forgotten. He at once commenced a picture of immense size—the taking of Smala, which in eight months he finished.

The repose of Horace Vernet is in his travels, and he is one of the greatest of modern travelers. It is said that the Arabian tribes love and respect him, and that he returns gladly to their society whenever duty requires it.

Horace Vernet has been blessed with but one child, a daughter, who married Paul Delaroche, a distinguished artist. This only child died in 1846.

In the later revolutions which have passed over France, Vernet has not participated. He has lived only in his profession and among his personal friends. He resided for years at Versailles, where he had a splendid mansion, but he removed to Paris a few years since. He is one of the greatest of modern artists, and is revered as an honor to the nation.

E*

EMILE DE GIRARDIN.

Girardin has been for so many years one of the leading minds of Paris, has been so distinguished as a journalist, that I have thought a slight sketch of his life and character would be acceptable to my readers.

It is said that he never knew the day of his birth, but it occurred in the year 1802. He does not appear to be as old as he in reality is, for his forehead is unwrinkled, his eye sparkles with a fascinating fire, and his hair is not gray. He carries almost always an eye-glass, which gives him the reputation—undeserved—of impertinence. His manners are those of a gentleman of the most refined cast, and, as editor of *La Presse*, he has long wielded a powerful influence over a class of minds.

Girardin was the illegitimate child of a count of the empire; his mother, taking advantage of the absence of her husband from France, conducted herself in a shameful manner with her lovers, and before her husband had returned, she had presented one of them with the subject of this sketch. Many scandalous stories have been coined by the enemies of Girardin respecting his birth, but the facts we have stated are undeniable. He was placed out at nurse with a woman named Choiseul, who took illegitimate children to the number of ten, from the wealthy and high-born, to care for and nurse. Had it not been for the shrewdness of this old nurse, Girardin would never have known his parents. For a time they came to see their child, in stolen visits, but gradually their visits died away, and were finally given up altogether. But the nurse in her walks about the streets met and recognized the familiar faces of the parents, and ascertained their condition in life.

The father was at this time unmarried, but at the instigation of his master, Napoleon, he wedded a young wife, and soon neglected his illegitimate child. Fearing that his wife would discover his secret, and take revenge upon him, he had the boy secretly removed to the care of an old servant of his, who was furnished with the means to take care of him and teach him all he knew himself, which was but little. He was strictly enjoined to call the child *Emile Delamothe.* This occurred in 1814. The father now thought that he had acquitted himself of his duty to the boy, and cared no more for him. But he was not blessed in his union—he had no legitimate children.

The man into whose care Emile was given, was a harsh

man, and gave the youth no rest from his severe discipline. He allowed him none of the pastimes of other children, and under this régime he suffered. At fourteen he had bad health, and a bilious color overspread his face, which never left it. Seeing that his health was suffering, the master sent him, under the care of his brother, into Normandy. This brother was a kind old soul, and gave the boy pleasant words, and a healthy, homely fare. In the country Emile enjoyed himself heartily. He wandered among the fields, played among the animals, and slept at night upon a litter of straw, and grew well again. In his ramblings he was oftenest alone, and pondered over his wretched fortunes. At eighteen he left the country for Paris. His first care was to visit his old nurse, and try to discover the condition of his parents. She could only give him a clew, but there had been such great changes since he left Paris, that she had no idea where his father dwelt, if he was alive. Emile then went to see the old man who first had care of him—his guardian—and plied him with questions. But he was impenetrable, and would reveal nothing. More than this—he read the law respecting illegitimate children, to Emile. It was a heavy blow upon his hopes. His guardian showed him proof of his birth, and a paper which gave to him, at twenty-one, the command of a small sum of money, the interest of which had heretofore supported him. In his anger he tore up the proof of his birth. Perhaps naturally, he at once took up against the laws of marriage, and became a bitter reformer. He frequented a reading-room, where he met several literary men who were in the habit of speaking of their books with pride. Emile was excited to try his own capabilities, and soon presented to his friends the manuscript of *Emile*, a story, the principal parts of which were true records of his own life. The literary friends were at variance in their criticisms upon the manuscript. Some declared it worthless, and advised him to get a style, while others praised the effort. Finding no publisher, our hero learned from a court directory the secret he had struggled after so long—the address of his father—and sent to him his story, written in a manner calculated to move the paternal heart. He received no direct reply, but eight days after, he was presented with an excellent situation with the secretary of Louis XVIII. Undoubtedly he was indebted to his father's recommendation for the place. So his story—afterward published—though it did not appear as he had intended when he wrote it, was not without its effect.

His time not being wholly occupied in the bureau, Girardin employed his spare moments in writing one or two novels, which appeared some time afterward. He has not been a voluminous author, *Emile* being his principal book. But his career has been that of a journalist, and though he has been everything by turns, yet he has had fame and influence.

By a turn in the wheel of fortune Girardin lost his place with the secretary, and went upon the exchange and solicited an humble office for the purpose of studying the chances there. As soon as he considered himself fit to decide, he ventured in buying very heavily certain stocks, and lost nearly all his little property. He was in despair and wrote to his father, who sent back an unfeeling letter. It is told of him that he presented himself before his father with a loaded pistol in either hand, and threatened to shoot him, and then himself, if he would not give him his name. This tale was undoubtedly invented by his enemies. He tried to enter the army but was rejected on account of his sickly appearance. He was so discouraged at this, that he attempted to commit suicide, and was saved from death as it were by a miracle. He resolved never again to give way to a similar rashness, and tried once more to succeed in life. He boldly took the name of Girardin, and though it was against law, yet his father feared scandal too much to institute legal measures against him. He now offered his book—*Emile*—to the publishers. It was eagerly caught up and sold rapidly. In the midst of his success he went to the minister and demanded employment, naming his father as reference! This bold application was successful, and he had a sinecure given him, as a kind of inspector of the fine arts.

He started a weekly journal with a friend, which was made up of selections. It was called *The Voleur*, and at the end of a month had a circulation of ten thousand. It was a dishonest mode of getting money, as no original writing was given. The name, *Voleur*, means thief. One of the authors whose writings were often quoted from in the *Voleur*, loudly remonstrated against the injustice of the procedure, and gaining no satisfaction, he fought a duel with Girardin, who was wounded in the shoulder, but the wound was not dangerous. It was not his first duel—he had fought with pistols in 1825. He withdrew from the conductorship of the *Voleur*, and under the patronage of the duchess de Berri, started a new journal, called *la Mode*. It had a great success, but as it waxed more and more liberal, the duchess repented her patronage, and finally withdrew it. The act gave the journal three thousand new subscribers. He foresaw the revolution of 1830, and sold out both his journals, thus taking excellent care of his property. Under the new *régime* he started a weekly paper, which acquired a circulation of one hundred and twenty thousand copies. He soon fell in love with Madamoiselle Delphine Gay, a talented and beautiful young woman, and married her.

After his marriage Girardin for several years turned his attention more particularly to philanthropic projects, which should benefit the people. He advocated savings banks, and gave much of his time to their establishment. He also founded an agricultural school. His wife turned him somewhat from his political and speculative plans, to more practical ones of this kind.

In 1833 he started *le Musee des Familles*, and to get subscribers, he placarded the walls of Paris with monstrous bills, initiating a nuisance which has ever since been used by all kinds of impostors. In 1834 he was elected to the Chamber of Deputies, and a year later he fought his third duel.

In 1836 *La Presse* was established, the journal with which his greatest fame is connected. In starting this new paper Girardin intended to ruin all the other Paris journals. His plan was to furnish more matter for one-half the ordinary price of a journal than the usual dailies gave to their readers. He made, as he might have expected, bitter enemies out of his cotemporaries. They attacked him, and with such unfairness, and in such a personal manner, that he flew to the courts for relief, or revenge. The journalists then accused him of cowardice—of fearing to trust his reputation to public discussion. It was at this time that he had his sad and fatal quarrel with Armand Carrel—a brother editor. Girardin shot Carrel in the groin. He died the next day. Girardin was wounded in the thigh. The loss of Carrel was deeply felt, and his funeral was attended by multitudes of the Parisians. For a time Girardin was exceedingly unpopular in Paris, and his enenies knew well how to make use of his unpopularity. They attacked him with redoubled severity and criticised all his questionable acts. He, however, replied to their fire with so much spirit, and with such terrible bitterness, that they were in the end if not conquered, willing to let him alone.

In his journal Girardin defended the throne, and was generally the friend of good morals. He is accused of signing his own name to all the most brilliant articles which appeared in his journal, whether he was in reality the author or not, for the sake of his reputation. He made enemies in all quarters, but his paper gained an immense circulation. His wife became his disciple, and rendered him great assistance in his literary labors. She has rendered her own name illustrious in France by her writings. She was entirely devoted to her husband, and not only loved the man but espoused his cause and principles. Whenever her husband was attacked she resented it, and often used a bitter and witty pen in his defense. Her verses upon Cavaignac are yet remembered in Paris. When that general arrested her husband, she flew to his house and demanded if she were living in the reign of terror.

"No," replied Cavaignac, "but under the reign of the sword."

"Attach a cord to your sword and you will be a guillotine!" replied the intrepid woman.

The drawing-rooms of Madame Girardin were among the most celebrated of the French capital. There might be seen the most distinguished authors, political celebrities, and soldiers of the time, and she was the leading spirit among them. Her husband rarely condescended to attend their *reünions*, as he had no taste for society and conversation. In the late revolutions which have swept over France, Girardin continued to save himself from exile or imprisonment. The truth is, he always loved money and power too well to make a sacrifice of himself for the cause of the people, and his course has been too much that of a demagogue from the first. His great object, during the latter part of his life, seems to have been to gain the portfolio of a minister—and without success, for from the days of the 1848 revolution, his influence rapidly declined.

VICTOR HUGO.

France has given birth to few men, in modern times, who exceed Victor Hugo in all that is noble and great. He is not simply a man of genius, a poet, and an orator, he is in its full sense *a man*. Too many of the brilliant men of France have lacked principle, have been ready to sell themselves to the highest bidder. It has not been so with Victor Hugo, and for that reason he is now an exile from the shores of his native land. His passionately eloquent orations, delivered on various sad occasions since he was exiled, have awakened the interest of the world, and people who cared little for him as the successful author, feel a deep sympathy for the noble exile.

Victor Hugo was born at Besançon in 1803, and of a

..ᴀı tamily. His father was a general in the service of Joseph Bonaparte, who was then king of Naples. He followed him into Spain, where he distinguished himself by his valor. He returned in 1814, and journeyed through Italy. Victor was then very young, but accompanied his father on his Italian tour. When but fourteen years old, Victor wrote a poem, to compete with many older persons for a prize, and though his poem was undoubtedly deserving of the reward, yet from his extreme youth, only honorable mention was made of his effort. This early poetical ambition, however, was an indication of his future career.

When he was twenty-two years of age, Charles X. gave him an audience, and Victor Hugo presented his majesty with some of his poetry. The king handed it to Chateaubriand, who was near, and demanded his opinion.

"Sire," said he, "the youth has a sublime genius!"

Hugo was displeased with the judgment of the Academy, which had not given him the prize for his first verses, and he wrote for an Academy at Toulouse, won several prizes, and was honored with a degree in the presence of Chateaubriand. He lived during this time in Paris, with his mother, who loved him to idolatry, and the affection was as warmly returned on the part of her son. She was a royalist and suggested his first poems. When she died he was overwhelmed with grief, and wrote a sad romance entitled *Han d' Glande*, which was severely attacked by the critics, many of whom knew his youth. But he triumphed over them all, as genuine genius is always sure to do. He now fell in love with a beautiful young girl, named Mademoiselle Foucher, and they married. He was twenty, and she was but fifteen years of age. They loved each other fondly, and if they were poor in gold, they were "very rich in virtues."

The publisher who brought out Hugo's romance, says that he visited the young family to purchase the second edition, and found them living in a pleasant little dwelling with two children to grace their fireside. Here came troops of friends, for Hugo had already made them among the wise and great. The politicians of the day, Thiers and others, were his companions. He often took his wife and children and went out to saunter in the public gardens or on the Boulevards, and wherever they went they carried happiness with them.

Hugo was still a royalist. It was more a sentiment than a principle with him, for he had not yet regarded politics with conscientious study. In 1826 a publisher made a collection of his poems, and issued them in one volume. It brought him wealth and renown. But though all this while Hugo was very happy in his family, yet the critics were bitter in their attacks upon him. He was accused of plagiarism, and especially when a new romance of his came out, he was accused of stealing it from Walter Scott.

The poet lost his first-born, and Madame Hugo took it so much to heart that he thought it wise to close their residence. Besides, changes had been made in the street so as to render it less pleasant as a residence. After one or two changes he finally settled down in the Place Royale, where he spent many years of his life. This dwelling was furnished to suit the taste of a poet, and was beautiful in every respect. It was filled with statues, paintings, and exquisite furniture, and his study, especially, was a charming apartment. Here his friends came—and they were numerous as the leaves upon a tree. Young authors flocked to his rooms and received counsel, and old men came to enjoy his conversation.

He next published *The Last days of the Condemned, and Notre Dame de Paris*, which had a fine success, and covered his name with glory in France. He now wrote *Marion Delorme* for the theater, but the censor would not allow it to be played. The king himself was appealed to, and confirmed the decision of his officer, and it appeared after his fall. This was the play which Dumas stole. When this play was rejected by the censor, Hugo wrote another for the theatrical manager who had engaged it, entitled *Hernani*, which had a splendid success. The opposition which he met from the actors and actresses was at first great, but he conquered all obstacles. The king, as if to appease him for the conduct of his censor, gave him a pension of six thousand francs a year, but he nobly refused to take a franc of it.

The success of *Delorme* was very great, and the Parisian public wept over it in dense crowds. One peculiarity of Hugo has been, that having once written a book or play he never recalls a sentence. Not to please managers, censors, or friends even, has he ever recalled a line, though it were to save himself from severe penalties. He has always been too proud and too conscientious to stoop in this way to either the populace or the government. In the meantime his house was besieged with publishers and theatrical managers, who besought him to use his pen for them.

He wrote, when once at a piece of work, with rapidity, and applied himself very closely. In writing *Notre Dame*, he was occupied for six months, and during that time he did not leave his house for a day, such were the urgent demands of his publisher upon him. He wrote for his publishers and for the managers and constantly increased his reputation. *Lucretia Borgia* appeared on the stage and had an almost unheard of success. It eclipsed all of his plays which had preceded it. He also published two or three volumes of songs at this time, which were enthusiastically received by the French people. He was always the warm friend of the poor. In 1834 he petitioned the duke of Orleans in favor of a poor family he chanced to know, and the duke gave a hundred louis to relieve them. In return the poet addressed the duke in song.

The manager who had brought out *Lucretia Borgia* offered him ten thousand francs for another, and very soon *Marie Tudor* made its appearance. There seems to have been trouble in its representation, from quarrels between rival actors. The manager acted dishonorably toward the poet. He announced his new play in an objectionable manner. Hugo complained, and he promised amendment the next day. But when the next day's announcement came Hugo saw no change, and what was worse still, the manager tried to deceive him by asserting that the bills were altered according to his wish. Hugo upbraided him for his falsehood, and demanded the play back. The manager would not give it up, for he had announced it. Said he:

"To-morrow your play will appear, and I will cause it to prove a failure."

"Instead of that," replied Hugo, "I will make your theater bankrupt."

The representation came on, and it proved eminently successful. But Hugo would not forgive such deception and insolence. He wrote a new play—*Angelo*—for a rival theater. In vain the old manager offered a high price for it. In a few months he and his theater were bankrupt, and he found, too late, that it was unwise to attempt to deceive and insult a man like Victor Hugo.

It is said that M. Hugo has a talent of high order for music, and also for drawing. During the cholera of 1832, he filled an album with caricatures to amuse his wife and children, and draw their attention from the dreadful ravages of the epidemic.

In 1841 Victor Hugo was elected a member of the Academy. Two years later he was raised to the dignity of peer of the realm. The duke of Orleans congratulated him upon the event.

A short time previous to this, Barbes was condemned to death. An application for a reprieve had been made to the king without being granted. A sister of Barbes came to Hugo, and besought him to use his influence with the king. Marie Wirtemburg had just died and the count de Paris was but a few weeks old. Hugo addressed a few touching lines of poetry to the king, and with allusions to the dead and the newly born, besought a pardon. It was instantly granted.

The history of Hugo from this time forward the whole world knows. He was an honest and hearty reformer. He was not content with glory as a man of letters—he wished to be of service to his suffering fellow-men. He was to a certain extent a communist, and a thorough republican. He hated the man Louis Napoleon, and was exiled. Belgium would not hold him, nor London—the latter was too full of smoke and fog to be endured. He said, after trying London, "The good Lord will not take the sunshine, too, from us."

He lives now in the island of Jersey, in a simple English mansion, but very comfortable. Behind it there is a beautiful garden terminated by a terrace, upon which the sea lashes its foam when the wind is high. From the window the sad exile beholds the distant shores of his native France.

In his retreat he has occupied himself with literary labors. He has been writing a volume of poetry to appear in the epic form. He has also been busy upon a volume of philosophy, a drama of five acts in which Mazarin is to figure as the principal character, two volumes of lyrical poetry, and a romance upon a modern subject, for which he has been offered one hundred and twenty thousand francs.

Madame Hugo and the children partake of exile with Victor Hugo, together with ten grandchildren. Charles Hugo, his son, who is with him, is distinguished as an author, but busies himself principally on the island in taking daguerreotype views. He has already made a hundred different pictures of his illustrious father, and sent them to his admirers in France.

Victor Hugo is a little over fifty years of age, and is full of life and animation. Let us hope that by political changes, or the clemency of the tyrant who sits upon the French throne, that he may soon return to the land he loves so well.

JULES JANIN.

"Oh! what a year in which to be born!" exclaims Janin of the year 1804—the year in which Napoleon, conqueror at the Pyranids and Marengo, placed upon his head the imperial crown—and the year which gave birth to the prince of French critics—Jules Janin. His parents were poor and humble, but honest and intelligent, and resided in Saint Etienne, near Lyons. At Lyons he entered school and became distinguished. At fifteen he imagined himself well versed in Greek and Latin, and in short, was a young egotist. His family fostered this self-love. An uncle said, "Let me send the prodigy to college in Paris!" An aunt paid the expenses of the first year—for he entered the college of Louis-le-Grand. This aunt loved the boy dearly, and for a week before he left, could not see him, such was her tenderness.

The whole family expected great things of him, and thought that his talents would be immediately recognized.

But they were doomed to disappointment. He gained no prize in college, and no honors. His aunt had expected that after one year, such were his talents, that the college would gladly give him the rest of his education, but she was obliged to support him for two years more.

He made himself unpopular with his teachers in college from fighting the Jesuits. When he left college he would not return to Saint Etienne, where his companions would mock him. He resolved to stay in Paris, even if he starved. He wrote to his kind old aunt, who at once came to Paris and made a quiet home for him. But this would not do—the rent of the house was half her income. He first took a class of pupils and taught them Latin, Greek, and history. This was a slight addition to their income. Summer came and his pupils left. He now was forced to engage with a professor of a boarding-school, at the rate of ten dollars a month, to teach. The professor was unfortunate and his furniture was attached, he, at the time, owing Jules for three months' work. He was an honest and good man, and Jules offered to give him the sum due, though he had not money enough left to get him a dinner. But he contrived a plan by which he cheated the law officers of a part of their goods, and got his pay. He was noted at this time more for his appetite than anything else, and would sacrifice more for a good dinner, probably, than for aught else. But in the absence of good living he took to solitary reading, and acquired a taste for literature.

He one day chanced to meet a college-friend who was a journalist.

"I am miserable," said Janin.

"Become a journalist, then," the friend replied, "if you have not an income"

That very night he was invited to dine with his friend, and made his resolution to live by his pen. He commenced his articles in the journals, writing at first criticisms upon theatrical performances. He at once commenced his system of flattering those who paid him well either in praise or gold, and denouncing authors and actors who were independent of him.

His kind aunt now died, after having expended her last franc, and Janin took up a new residence. He soon acquired such fame in his critical writings, that he was at ease. He engaged with the *Figaro* journal, and contributed powerfully to its success. He was, of course, wel. paid for his services. He fell in love with a young girl in humble life. An artist did the same. The two men quarreled about her, and Janin wrote a book in which the woman was the heroine. But he was unsuccessful—the young woman married the painter and was happy. Janin rose to the highest position as a fashionable critic in Paris, and still he has never acquired beyond France the reputation of a profound critic and scholar.

In October, 1841, he was married, and instead of spending a pleasant evening, he celebrated his marriage by going to his room and writing a newspaper article, greatly to his prejudice amongst his friends. Of late it has been remarked, that Jules Janin is less imperious in his criticisms than he was formerly. He has been very severely reviewed by Dumas and Roqueplan, and has behaved more wisely since.

We have not sketched Jules Janin as a great man, but as a man who makes great pretensions, and who has long been acknowledged. in Paris and France, as the prince of critics.

CHAPTER VI.

PLACES OF BLOOD—PLACE DE LA CONCORDE.

Almost every fine square in Paris has a high-sounding name. For instance, that spot which has been the theater of so much tragedy, upon which so much human blood has been poured, is called the *Place de la Concorde.* It much more appropriately might be called the Place of Blood. So there are other, many other spots in Paris, which deserve a scarlet title, and when wandering a stranger through its streets, whenever I came to one of these, I was strongly inclined to stop and indulge in reverie. The past history of France and Paris arose before my mind, and I could not, if I would, away with it. The characters who acted parts in Paris and perished in those places were before me, and their histories lent a powerful interest to the spot upon which they suffered and died. The reader can have no adequate idea of the feelings with which a stranger visits these places of sad memories, unless he recalls them to mind, nor will it be out place for me to do so.

A prison was often pointed out to me in which the celebrated Madame Roland was confined, and the spot upon which she suffered death. I gazed long at the grim walls which shut out the sunlight from that noble woman—long upon the stones which drank her blood in the Place de la Concorde. Her whole history was as vividly before me as if I were living in the terrible days of blood. Her maiden name was Manon Philipon, and her father was an engraver. They lived in Paris, where she grew up with the sweetest of dispositions, and one of the finest of intellects. Her mother was a woman of refinement and culture. She was excessively fond of books and flowers, so much so that many years later she wrote, "I can forget the injustice of men and my sufferings, among books and flowers." Her parents gave her good masters, and she applied herself to her studies with ardor and delight. They were never harsh in their treatment of her, but always gentle and kind. She acted nearly as she pleased, but seems not to have been spoiled by such a discipline as we might have expected. When she was only nine years old, Plutarch fell into her hands, and she was intensely interested in it—more so than with all the fairy tales she had ever read. From him she drank in republicanism at that early age. She also read Fenelon and Tasso. She spent nearly the whole of her time in reading, though she assisted her mother somewhat in her household duties. The family belonged to the middle-classes, and despised the debaucheries of the higher and lower orders of the people. The mother was pious, and Manon was placed for a year in a convent. She then spent a year with her grandparents, and returned to her father's house. Her course of reading was very much enlarged, and her attention was now specially directed to philosophical works. She was thus a great deal alone, and gave little of her time to gossip and promenade. She went, however, once to Versailles, and saw the routine of court, but returned with a great delight to her old books and the heroes in them. She was dissatisfied with France and Frenchmen. She says: "I sighed as I thought of Athens, where I could have equally admired the fine arts without being wounded by the spectacle of despotism. I transported myself in thought to Greece—I was present at the Olympic games, and I grew angry at finding myself French. Thus struck by all of grand which is offered by the republics of antiquity, I forgot the death of Socrates, the exile of Aristides, the sentence of Phocion."

She began, at last, to repine at her situation. She felt conscious of her abilities, and that her thoughts were high and noble, and she longed for a higher position, in which she might use her talents. Her father grew more and more poor and unable to care for his family, and her mother was anxious that she should be married. She did not lack offers. She was beautiful and accomplished, and many suitors presented themselves, but not one whom she could love. Her mother now died, to her great sorrow. She now persuaded her father to retire from the business which he was ruining, and save the little property he had left, and she retired to a little convent. She prepared her own food, lived very simply, and saw only her own relations.

It was about this time that Manon became acquainted, through a school-friend, with M. Roland, who was the younger son of a poor, but noble family, and whose lot in life was not an easy one. He was now considerably advanced in years, and was superintendent of the manufactories at Rouen and Amiens. He had written several works upon these subjects, and was somewhat celebrated. She took great pleasure in his society, and after five years of friendship, respected, and perhaps loved him. He offered himself and was finally accepted. She says: "In short, if marriage was as I thought, an austere union, an association in which the woman usually burdens herself with the happiness of two individuals, it were better that

I should exert my abilities and my courage in so honorable a task, than in the solitude in which I lived."

The married couple visited Switzerland and England, and then settled down near Lyons, with her husband's relations. She had one child—a daughter—and her life and happiness consisted in taking care of her and her husband. She thus gives a beautiful picture of her life:

"Seated in my chimney corner at eleven, before noon, after a peaceful night and my morning tasks—my husband at his desk, and his little girl knitting—I am conversing with the former, and overlooking the work of the latter; enjoying the happiness of being warmly sheltered in the bosom of my dear little family, and writing to a friend, while the snow is falling on so many poor wretches overwhelmed by sorrow and penury. I grieve over their fate, I repose on my own, and make no account of those family annoyances which appeared formerly to tarnish my felicity."

The revolution came amid all their sweet and quiet pleasure, but found her ready for it. M. Roland was elected to the National Assembly, to represent Lyons. The family at once repaired to Paris, and the house of Roland was at once the rendezvous for the talented, the men of genius, but more especially the Girondists, as th more conservative of the republicans were called. The genius and beauty of Madame Roland soon became known, and made her house the fashionable resort of the *elité* of Paris. The arrest of the king filled her with alarm. She was not willing to push matters to such extremes. She was one of the noblest of republicans, out sne was merciful and moderate in some of her views. Her husband again retired to the country—to Lyons. Amid the solitude of their own home she grew discontented. She could not, having tasted the sweets of life in Paris, abandon it without a pang of sorrow. The following winter a new ministry was formed of the Girondists, and her husband was named minister for the interior. They again returned to Paris, and now in greater state. Roland was one of the most honest men of the revolution, but was so precise and methodical in his papers which were prepared for the public, that without the assistance of his wife, his success would have been far less than it was.

M. Roland wishing to save the king, if possible, determined upon remonstrating with him upon his course. Madame Roland wrote the letter of remonstrance, though, of course, it appeared in his name. It was bold and severe, and accomplished no good. The result of it was, that Roland was dismissed from the office, and retired to private life. Soon after, however, he was recalled under the republic, and endeavored to do his duty. Madame Roland writes in September of this year: "We are under the knife of Marat and Robespierre. These men agitate the people and endeavor to turn them against the National Assembly." She and her husband were heartily and zealously for the republic, but they were moderate, and entirely opposed to those brutal men who were in favor of filling Paris and France with blood. Madame Roland writes, later: "Danton leads all; Robespierre is his puppet; Marat holds his torch and dagger: this ferocious tribune reigns, and we are his slaves until the moment when we shall become his victims. You are aware of my enthusiasm for the revolution: well, I am ashamed of it; it is deformed by monsters and become hideous." Madame Roland now struggled to otherthrow the Jacobins—but was only overthrown herself. She was at this time celebrated for her wit and beauty. A writer of that time says of her:

"I met Madame Roland several times in former days: her eyes, her figure, and hair, were of remarkable beauty; her delicate complexion had a freshness and color which, joined to her reserved yet ingenuous appearance, imparted a singular air of youth. Wit, good sense, propriety of expression, keen reasoning, *naive* grace, all flowed without effort from her roseate lips."

During the horrible massacres of September Roland acted with great heroism. While the streets of Paris ran with human blood, he wrote to the mayor, demanding him to interfere in behalf of the sufferers. Marat denounced him as a traitor, and from that moment his life was in danger. Madame Roland was charged with instigating the unpopular acts of her husband by the radicals, and she was in equal danger with her husband. After the execution of the king, Roland became discouraged, and convinced that he could do no more for France, and he retired with his wife to the country. Here they lived in constant danger of arrest. Roland finding the danger so great, made good his escape, but she was arrested a short time after. She had retired to rest at night, when suddenly her doors were burst open and the house filled with a hundred armed men. She was instantly parted from her child and sent off to Paris. One of the men who had her in charge, cried out, "Do you wish the window of the carriage to be closed?" "No, gentlemen," she replied, "innocence, however oppressed, will never assume the appearance of guilt. I fear the eyes of no one, and will not hide myself."

She was shut up in prison at once. She asked for books —for Plutarch, and Thompson's Seasons. On the 24th of

June she was liberated, and then suddenly reärrested. This deception was more than cruel, it was infamous. She was placed in the prison of St. Pelaige—a filthy and miserable place. The wife of the jailor pitied her and gave her a neat, upper apartment, and brought her books and flowers, and she was comparatively happy again. It was in this prison that she wrote her own memoirs. She usually kept a stout heart, but at times when thoughts of her husband and child came over her, she was overwhelmed with grief.

The chief Girondists now began to fall under the stroke of the guillotine, and her turn was quickly coming. The day that her friend Brissot perished, she was transferred to the *Conciergerie*, the prison which suggested this sketch of her to my mind. I went over this prison, and the very apartment was pointed out to me in which Madame Roland was confined. Here she spent her last days, and wretched days they were, indeed. But she conducted herself nobly and courageously through all. The mockery of a trial was held, and she wrote her own defense, a most eloquent production. She was sentenced to death in twenty-four hours. Twenty-two victims had just poured out their blood, and she was to follow their example. A French writer speaks of her at that time as " full of attractions, tall, of an elegant figure, her physiognomy animated, but sorrow and long imprisonment had left traces of melancholy on her face that tempered her natural vivacity. Something more than is usually found in the eyes of woman, beamed in her large, dark eyes, full of sweetness and expression. She often spoke to me at the grate, with the freedom and courage of a great man. This republican language falling from the lips of a pretty French woman, for whom the scaffold was prepared, was a miracle of the revolution. We gathered attentively around her in a species of admiration and stupor. Her conversation was serious, without being cold. She spoke with a purity, a melody, and a measure which rendered her language a soul of music of which the ear never tired. She spoke of the deputies who had just perished with respect, but without effeminate pity; reproaching them even for not having taken sufficiently strong measures. Sometimes her sex had mastery, and we perceived that she had wept over the recollection of her daughter and husband."

She was led out to execution on the 10th of November, on that place of blood—*La Concorde*. She was dressed in white, and inspired the multitudes who saw her with admiration. Another victim accompanied her. She exhorted him to ascend first, that his courage might not be shaken by witnessing her death. She turned to the statue of Liberty, exclaiming, "Oh, Liberty! how many crimes are committed in thy name." She was thirty-nine years of age, and though she ended her life thus young, she had achieved immortality.

M. Roland was at this time in safety in Rouen, but when he heard of the death of his noble wife, he resolved to give himself up at once to the authorities. The interests of his child, however, tempted him to another course. Should he give himself up he would certainly perish, and by the law of France his possessions would be confiscated, and would not, therefore, descend to his child. Were he to die, even by his own hand, the case would be different —he would save the property for his child. Five days after his wife perished upon the scaffold, he fell upon his sword on a high road near Rouen. The following lines were found upon his person:

"The blood that flows in torrents in my country dictates my resolve: indignation caused me to quit my retreat. As soon as I heard of the murder of my wife, I determined no longer to remain on an earth tainted by crime."

I had occasion often while in Paris to cross the street of the *Ecole de Medicine.* It is a rather pleasant street, and leads into the street of *Ancienne Comedie,* named so after the *Theater Francaise,* which was formerly located upon it. Just opposite it is a *café* which Voltaire used to frequent, and I have stopped to take a cup of chocolate in it. But one day I hunted up number eighteen of the street of *Ecole de Medicine.* The house was one which Marat used to occupy in the time of the great revolution. We paused a moment upon the threshold, and then passed up a flight of stairs and entered the room where Marat used to write so many of his blood-thirsty articles. A little room at that time opened out of it, and in the apartment was a bath-room. He often wrote in his bath in this room.

The last day Marat lived, was the 13th of July, 1793, and it was spent in this little room. He was the monster of the revolution, loved the sight of blood as a tiger does, and his influence over the multitude gave him power to sacrifice whoever he pleased. If he but pointed his long finger at a man or woman, it was death to the victim. No one was safe. Under his devilish prompting, already some of the truest republicans in France had been beheaded, and every hour some unfortunate man or woman fell beneath his hellish ferocity. Should a fiend be allowed to personate liberty longer? Should a wretch whose very touch scorched and blistered, whose breath was that of the lake of fire, any longer be allowed to pollute France with his presence? These were the questions which presented themselves to the mind of a young country-girl. Who would have thought that the young and beautiful Charlotte Corday would have taken it upon herself to answer these questions and avenge the murdered innocents?

She had learned to love, to adore liberty, among the forests and hills of her native country. She saw Marat perpetrating murders of the blackest die in the name of liberty. He went further still, he sacrificed her friends—the friends of liberty. She resolved that *the wretch should die.* No one could suspect the dark-haired girl. Enthusiastic to madness, she flew to Paris with but one thought filling her breast—that she was amid the terrors of that time, in the absence of all just law, commanded by God to finish the course of Marat. Everything bent to this idea. She cared nothing for her own life—nothing for her own happiness. She came to the threshold of the house many a time and was turned away—she could not gain admittance. Marat's mistress was jealous of him, and Charlotte Corday had heard of this and feared that it would be impossible to see him alone. She therefore wrote to the monster, and with great eloquence demanded a private interview. The request was granted.

On the morning of the 13th of July she came in person, and Marat ordered that she be shown into his room. He lay in his bath, with his arms out of water, writing. He looked up at her as she entered, and asked her business. She used deception with him, declaring that some of his bitterest enemies were concealed in the neighborhood of her country home. She named, with truth, some of her dearest friends as these enemies. "They shall die within forty-eight hours," said Marat. This was enough—in an instant she plunged a dagger, which she had concealed about her person, to the center of his heart.

She was executed for this deed upon the *Place de la Concorde.* They tell the story in France, to show how modest she was, that after her head had fallen from the body a rough man pushed it one side with his foot, *and her cheeks blushed scarlet.* Marat was interred with great pomp in the Pantheon, but a succeeding generation did better justice to his remains, for they were afterward, by order of government, disinterred and thrown into a common sewer. I scarcely ever stopped on the *Place de la Concorde* without thinking of Charlotte Corday, and bringing up the dreadful scene in Marat's house, and her own execution. I fancied her as she appeared that day—a smile upon her face, a wild enthusiastic joy in her eyes, as if she had executed her task, and was willing, glad, to leave such a horror-stricken land. No man can doubt the purity of Charlotte Corday's character. She was no ordinary murderer. She did not act from the promptings of anger, or to avenge private wrongs. She felt it to be her duty to rid France of such an unnatural monster, and undoubtedly thought herself God's minister of vengeance.

Another spot which may justly be denominated a place of blood, is the Conciergerie. It is yet as grim and awful as ever, in its appearance. The spot is still shown in the stones where the blood ran from the swords of the human butchers. If the history of this prison were written, it would make a dozen books, and some of the most heart-rending tragedies would be unfolded to the world. The great and good, and the wretchedly vile, have together lived within its walls and lost their hopes of life, or their desire for it. I could never pass it without a shudder, for though it was not so much a place of execution as a prison, yet so terrible a place was it that many a prisoner has joyfully emerged from its dark walls to the scaffold. It has witnessed the death of many a poor man and woman, stifled with its foul air, its horrid associations, and the future with which it terrified its inmates. Many a noble heart has been broken in its damp and dimly-lighted cells, for it has existed for many centuries. As early as 1400 it was the scene of wholesale butchery, and on St. Bartholomew's night, its bells rang out upon the shuddering air, to add their voice with the others, which filled every heart with fear.

Paris is one of the most singular cities in the civilized world for one thing—for the atrocities which it has witnessed. Certainly, in modern times no city in the world has been the scene of such hideous acts as the city of the fine arts. Deeds have been done within a century, which would put a savage to the blush. The place is still pointed out where a poor girl was burned by a slow fire. She had wounded a soldier, and as a punishment, she was stripped naked, her breasts cut off, her skin slashed by red hot sabres, while she was being burned. Her yells could be heard over half Paris.

Think, too, of later times—when Louis Napoleon aimed his cannon at the houses of inoffensive people, and shot down, in cold blood, some of the best inhabitants of Paris. A more hellish act was never perpetrated in this world of ours than that—yet he is the patron of modern civilization, and is on excellent terms with the amiable Queen Victoria. I do not wonder that Rosseau argued that the primitive and savage condition of man is to be preferred to French civilization. This is one phase of Paris life as it is to-day, and as it always has been, and it is right that the stranger should not pass it by.

Paris is crowded with such places as these I have been describing—spots to which bloody histories cling. The paving-stones are, as it were, red to this day with the blood they drank in the times of the revolution.

PLACE DE LA CONCORDE.

There is no public square or place in the world, which in broad magnificence surpasses the *Place de la Concorde.* The stranger can form little idea of it, except by personal inspection. Stand in the center and look which way you will, something grand or beautiful greets the eye. Look toward the south, and see the fine building which contains the senate chamber, the bridge over the Seine, and the *Quai de Orsay.* To the north, and see the row of buildings named Place de la Concorde, with their grand colonnades and the pretentious Madeleine. To the east, and there the green forest of the Tuileries gardens, with its rich array of flowers and statuary—and the palace—greets you, and farther away the grand towers of Notre Dame. Or look where the sun sets—the Elysian fields are all before you with their music and dancing and shows; their two long promenades, and in the distance Napoleon's grand triumphal arch.

To look at the Place de la Condorde itself, you should stand upon the bridge across the Seine—from its center look down upon the great open *plaza*, see the wonderful fountains, gaze up at the obelisk of Luxor in the center, and you will be struck with admiration of the grand scene before you.

But I confess that I was attracted to the Place de la

Concorde more by the historical associations connected with it, than by its present magnificence. Leaning upon the parapet of the bridge and looking down upon the Seine, a pleasant July morning was present to my imagination, and a crowd was gathered upon the place to witness an execution. The slight form of a beautiful woman passes up yonder winding steps to the block. Her hair is dark—not so dark, though, as her genius-lighted eyes—and her forehead is white and nobly pure. She kneels, bows down her head to the block, and is forever dead. It was Charlotte Corday, the enthusiast, who assassinated Marat in his bath. I have seen the place where she killed him—have looked at the very threshold where she waited so long before she gained admittance. The house is standing yet, and the room where Marat lay in his bath writing—where he looked up from his manuscript at Charlotte Corday and promised death to some of her dearest friends in a provincial town—where she plunged her dagger to the center of his black heart!

It was on the Place de la Concorde that Louis XVI. expiated the crimes of his ancestors upon the scaffold. One still October day the sweet though proud Marie Antoinette came here, also, to die. The agony that she suffered during her trial, and the day that she perished upon the scaffold, no human thought can reckon. The French revolution taught a fearful lesson to kings and queens; that if they would rule safely, it must be through the hearts of their subjects, otherwise the vengeance of an insulted and oppressed people will be sure to overtake them.

One April day, amid sunshine and rain, that man of dark eyes, lofty brow, and proud stature, the magnificent Danton, walked up the fatal steps and knelt down to death. How strange! The man before whose nod all Paris had trembled as if he had been a god—the man whose eloquence could thrill the heart of France, was now a weak creature beneath the iron arm of Robespierre He had sentenced hundreds to death upon this spot, and was now condemned himself, by his old associate, to taste the same bitter cup which he had so often held to the lips of others. This act alone will fix the stain of ferocious cruelty upon the character of Robespierre, however conscientious he may have been.

And here, too, on that same day, Camille Desmoulins, the mad author and revolutionist-editor, ended his young life. Many a time with his comic—yet sometimes awfully tragic—pen, had he pointed with laughter to the Place de la Concorde, and its streams of human blood. And now the strange creature who one day laughed wildly in his glee and another was all tears and rage, followed Danton, the man he had worshiped, to the block. Robespierre was his old friend, he had written his praises upon many a page, yet now he stood aloof, and raised not a hand to save the poor editor, though he besought his aid with passionate eloquence.

Three months later, and the Place de la Concorde witnessed the closing scene of the revolution. On the 28th of the following July, Robespierre and St. Just perished together on the scaffold. He whose very name, articulated in whispers, had made households tremble as with a death-ague, had lost his power, and was a feeble, helpless being. Cruel, stern, without a feeling of mercy in his heart, awful to contemplate in his steel severity, he was, after all, almost the only man of the revolution who was strictly, sternly, rigidly honest. No one can doubt his integrity. He might have been dictator if he would, and saved his life, but the principles which were a part of his very nature, would not allow him to accept such power, even from the people. His friends plead with streaming eyes; it was a case of life or death; but he said, "Death, rather than belie my principles!" and he perished.

As I looked down upon the very spot where stood the scaffold, and saw that all around was so peaceful, I could hardly realize that within half a century such a terrible drama had been enacted there—a drama whose closing acts illustrate the truth of that scripture which saith, "Whoso taketh the sword shall perish by the sword."

Louis XVI. first ascends the scaffold, looking mournfully at Danton, but saying never a word; and then Vergniaud, the pure of heart, executed by his friend Danton; then Danton, thinking remorsefully of Vergniaud and cursing Robepierre; and last, Robespierre!

The Place de la Concorde was originally an open spot, where were collected heaps of rubbish, but in 1763 the authorities of the city of Paris determined to clear it up and erect upon it a statue in honor of Louis XV. The statue was destroyed by the populace in 1792, and the place named *Place de la Revolution.* In 1800 it took the name it at present retains. In 1816 Louis XVIII. caused the statue of Louis XV. to be replaced, though still later that of Louis XVI. was erected here, and the former placed in the Champs Elysees.

The obelisk of Luxor is perhaps the most prominent feature of the place. It is a magnificent relic of Egypt, and is one of two obelisks which stood in front of the temple of Thebes. It was erected fifteen hundred and fifty years before Christ, by Sesostris, in the eighteenth Egyptian dynasty. Mehemet Ali made a present of the obelisk to the French government. On account of its enormous size, great difficulty was experienced in removing it to Paris. A road was constructed from the obelisk to the Nile, and eight hundred men were occupied three months in removing it to the banks of the river, where was a flat-bottomed vessel built expressly for it. A part of the vessel had to be sawed off to receive it, so great was its size. It descended the Nile, passed the Rosetta bar, and with great care was towed to Cherbourg. It must be remembered that the obelisk is a single stone, seventy-two feet high, and weighs five hundred thousand pounds. On the 16th of August, 1836, it was drawn up an inclined plane to the top of the pedestal where it now stands. In the following October, the public ceremony of placing it occurred, in the presence of the royal family, and more than a hundred and fifty thousand other persons.

Place de la Concorde.

The cost of removal from Thebes to Paris was two millions francs, but not a life was lost from the beginning to the end of the transaction. It stands upon a single block of gray granite, the total height of obelisk and pedestal being about a hundred feet.

There are two fountains upon the Place, dedicated, one to Maritime, the other to Fluvial navigation. The basin of each is fifty feet in diameter, out of which rise two smaller ones, the latter inverted. Six tall figures are seated around the larger basins, their feet resting on the prows of vessels, separated from each other by large dolphins which spout water into the higher basins. But the beauty of the Place de la Concorde is not so much the result of any one feature as the combination of the whole, and as such it is unequaled in Europe.

From the Place de la Concorde one has a fine view of the Arch of Triumph, which was erected by Napoleon in honor of his great victories.

CHAPTER VII.

THE LOUVRE—PUBLIC GARDENS—LUXEMBOURG PALACE AND GARDENS—THE GOBELINS.

THE LOUVRE.

THE subject is hackneyed and old—what can *I* say about the Louvre which will be new to the reader? However, to write a book on Paris, and make no mention of the Louvre, would be like acting the play of Hamlet, with Hamlet omitted. I make no pretensions to critical skill in reference to paintings or architecture, I only give the impressions of a man who loves both when they seem beautiful to him. I am no such art enthusiast that I love to wander through galleries of naked and sensual pictures, though they do show great genius. Nor can the glitter and grandeur of a thousand public buildings hide from my eyes the squalor and wretchedness of the common people.

I will not give a precise description of the Louvre, but record the things which struck me most forcibly.

The foreigner by showing his passport is admitted any day into the Louvre, though certain days are specified for the public to enter, and upon others the artists of Paris are busy in studying and copying the works of the masters.

It was one of those days, when the Louvre was occupied by the artists, that I presented my American passport at one of the entrances, and was politely invited to

THE LOUVRE.

pass in. My companion was a French artist, who had kindly offered to guide me over the renowned collection of paintings. The visit was much pleasanter to me from the fact that no crowd of visitors was present, and it was a novel sight to behold the young artists of Paris engaged in their work. I have mentioned in another part of this book that no pictures of living artists are allowed a place in the Louvre. The Luxembourg Gallery is the place for all such, and the Louvre collection is therefore made up of paintings from the hands of all the old masters. It is for this reason that the Parisian artists fill the rooms of the Louvre so constantly—either to copy some gem in the vast collection, or by practice, to catch some of the genius of the master-hand.

The first picture-room we entered is represented to be the finest for the exhibition of pictures in the world. Its splendor was really very great. The pictures in it are of immense size, and they require a strong and clear light. It is called the Grand Saloon, and is divided by projecting arcades which are supported by fine marble columns. The length is one thousand three hundred and twenty-two feet, and the breadth forty-two feet. The ceilings and the walls are completely covered by pictures, the number of them being one thousand four hundred. Those by French masters number three hundred and eighty, by the Flemish and German five hundred and forty, and by the Italian four hundred and eighty. The greater part of the collection was made by Napoleon, and though many of the finest pictures were taken away by the allies in 1815, yet it is still one of the largest collections in the world. To stand in this room and gaze at leisure upon some of the finest paintings in the world, was a delight I had never before felt. It is indescribable, yet it was none the less real. I could not, as my friend the artist did, point out the peculiar excellences of each, and the faults, nor compare one with another critically, but I could feel the same thrill of pleasure which he did, and I found that the picture which he declared to be the finest, was that before which I delayed longest. It certainly is no more necessary for a man to be an art-critic to love pictures, than it is to be a botanist to love flowers. I admit that one must be a critic, to a degree, to *thoroughly* appreciate the art of painting, but that is another thing. The common people in France are universally fond of pictures, much more so than the English. The Americans are next to the French in ideality, notwithstanding their great practicality. The common people of England are far behind those of America in their fondness for the beautiful—at least I judge so from a pretty fair experience. America as yet, to be sure, can show few works of art, but the vast number of enlightened Americans who continually visit Europe, and many for the purpose of seeing the grand and beautiful in art, tells the story. The English upper-classes are undoubtedly well-educated in art, but not the other classes. But I must not digress.

The second room we visited was the *Salle des Bijoux*, and was entirely occupied by vases, jewels, and rare and costly cups. I was much pleased with an Arabian basin of splendid workmanship. There were also articles of toilette given by the ancient republic of Venice to Marie de Medicis, one casket alone being worth many thousands of dollars.

The next apartment we entered contains copies of Raphael's frescoes in the Vatican at Rome; but the next room interested me more, for it contains Grecian statuary and antiquities. The southern part of Italy and Etruria, Her culaneum and Pompeii, are all represented in the collection. One striking feature of this hall is, that the ceilings are covered with paintings of the best artists. One represents Vesuvius receiving fire from Jupiter to consume Herculaneum and Pompeii; another, Cybele protecting the two cities from the fires of Vesuvius.

The *Hall du Trone*, which we next visited, contained a great variety of beautiful pictures. One is a representation of the Genius of Glory supported by Virtue, with a scroll on which are written the names of the heroes of France—the warriors, statesmen, and great writers. There are in this apartment many exquisite vases, and among them four of Sevres porcelain, and one of Berlin porcelain, a present from the king of Prussia. There are, also, two very fine Chinese side-boards and specimens of Chinese sculpture.

We next looked into the *Musee Egyptian*, which contains Egyptian curiosities, and the ceilings are painted, but, of course, by modern authors, as they are executed not upon canvas, but upon the hard ceiling. One of the paintings represents Egypt as being saved by Joseph—another, and one of the finest of the ceiling decorations in the Louvre, is by Horace Vernet. It represents Julian II. giving orders to Michæl Angelo, Raphael, and Bramante to construct St. Peters.

The *Galerie Francaise* is filled with paintings of the French school, but none of them are by living painters. Many of them are unquestionably fine specimens of art, but as they were principally portraits of men more distinguished by their position than by any genius, I was not interested in the collection.

Very near the French gallery, there is an alcove in which Henry IV. used often to to sleep, and where he at last died. His portrait is now exhibited in i.. In another little recess the suit of armor which Henry II. wore on the day of his death, is shown to the stranger. It was in the year 1559. The day was very hot and the king let down his helmet for fresh air. The royal party were engaged in a tournament, when the tilting-spear of the count de Montgomerie pierced the king's eye, and through it his brain, and he died.

The Spanish gallery contains many fine specimens of the works of the Spanish masters, Velasquez, Murillo, and others.

The Standish Collection is so called, because it was given to Louis Phillippe in 1838, by an Englishman by the name of Standish. It includes many first-class paintings, and a bible once owned by Cardinal Ximenes, now valued at twenty-five thousand francs. Before Louis Phillippe died, he claimed this collection as his private property. He had no intention of taking it away, but wished to test his claim to it. It was acknowledged, and he then bequeathed it to the Louvre.

It is impossible for me in a brief sketch to even mention *all* the apartments in the Louvre, and I must pass by many. The upper floor is devoted to a Marine museum. It contains fourteen rooms, all well-filled with curiosities. Among them I noticed some excellent models of brigs, ships, men-of-war, Chinese junks, etc. There is in this suite of rooms a fine display of American curiosities. It first struck me that Colton's collection must be before me, but I soon discovered my mistake.

The Louvre contains a spacious museum of antiquities beneath the painting-galleries. There is also a museum of modern sculpture on the ground-floor. It contains the finest specimens of French sculpture, as well as the master-pieces of foreign sculptors. In the first room there is one of Michael Angelo's best pieces—the Master and his Slave. It is, indeed, a master-piece. One of Canova's pieces—a Cupid and a Psyche—thrilled me with its exceeding beauty.

But I must say a few words respecting the building of the Louvre. The eastern facade is one of the finest specimens of architecture that any age can boast. The colonnade is composed of twenty-eight Corinthian columns. There is a gallery behind them in which you may promenade, looking out upon the streets below. The southern front of the Louvre, seen from one of the bridges of the river, with its forty Corinthian pilasters and sculptures, is a magnificent sight.

The building of the Louvre forms a perfect square, and after visiting the different galleries, the stranger will find that he has completed the circuit. The gateways are fine and richly ornamented with sculptures, and the court is a pleasant one. Each side of the building measures four hundred and eight feet.

In the year 1200, Phillip Augustus used a castle which existed on the present site of the Louvre, for a state prison. Charles V. made additions to the building and placed the Royal Library in it. The present building was begun by Francis I., in 1528, and the southern side of the Louvre as it now exists was his work. Henry II., Henry IV., and Louis XIII., successively added to it, and in still later time, Louis XIV., Louis XV., Charles X., Louis Phillippe, and Napoleon III., have done the same.

Charles X. stood in one of the windows of the Louvre overlooking the Seine, and fired upon the poor victims of the massacre of St. Bartholomew. In July, 1830, the people made a terrible attack upon it, and it was courageously defended by the Swiss Guards, until every one of them perished.

The Louvre is one of the noblest piles in Europe, and as a painting-gallery, it reflects great credit upon France. I used to frequent it, yet I must, to be honest, confess that many of its pictures are too sensual and licentious to suit my taste. Are such pictures as can be found in the French gallery, pictures which express sensuality and debauchery, productive of good?

Is it well to look at so much nakedness, even if it be executed with the highest art? In portions of the Louvre there is altogether too much nakedness, and I humbly hope that American ladies will never get so accustomed to such sights that they can stare at them in the presence of gentlemen without a blush. I now allude to the most licentious pictures in the collection. I saw French women stop and criticise pictures which I could not look at, in their presence, at least—pictures which exhibited the human form in a state of nudity, and at the same time expressed the most shameful sensuality and portrayed the most licentious attitudes. I cannot believe a woman of perfectly pure mind can delight to look at such pictures in a public gallery. But this nakedness is all of a piece with many other things which characterize French society, and but shows the corrupt state of the morals of the French people.

JARDIN DES TUILLERIES.

PUBLIC GARDENS.

The gardens of Paris are almost numberless. Some of them are free, and others are open only to those who pay an entrance fee. The latter class is great in numbers, from the aristocratic *Jardin d' Hiver* down to La Chaumiere. In the first you meet the fashionable and rich, and in the last, the students with their grisettes, and the still poorer classes. But I will not describe this class of gardens in this article.

The Tuileries gardens are perhaps as aristocratic as any in Paris, if that term can be appropriately applied to a *free* garden, and they are certainly among the finest in the world. They are filled with statues and fountains, trees and flowers. The western part is entirely devoted to trees, almost as thickly planted as our American forests. The care which is taken of this grove of trees surprised me, and I think would any new-world visitor. The trees grow closely to the southern wall of the gardens, yet do not protrude their branches over the line of the wall. The sight is a singular one from the banks of the Seine, outside the walls of the garden, for the whole grove looks exactly as if it had been *sheared* like a hedge. The branches have been so cared for and trimmed, that the side presented is perfectly even and a mass of green. Still this, though curious, is not beautiful. Trees need to grow naturally for that. Art cannot surpass nature in this way. The grove is full of beauty. Walks run every way over it, and the trees are so trimmed and cultivated that beautiful arches are formed over nearly all the paths. This constitutes the forest, one of the most singular in Paris, and it is a novel sight to the stranger. On the north side of the groves there is a collection of orange trees, and in among them are set a large quantity of chairs, which are rented by a person in attendance for two sous an hour. So for two cents, a man can sit and rest himself in one of the most delicious spots in Paris. This is a peculiar feature of all the gardens of Paris. No free seats are furnished, but an old woman is sure to select some shady and enchanting spot whereon to arrange her chairs, which are for rent. Indeed, there are many places on the Boulevard where this practice obtains, to the great joy of numberless tired pedestrians.

In front of the *Tuileries palace* there is a choice garden of flowers and plants enclosed by an iron railing. The flowers were in bloom when last I saw it, and were exceedingly beautiful. Directly in front of this garden a fine fountain is always playing, and scattered in every direction is a profusion of statuary. There are some magnificent groups, but again others are disgusting in their sensuality. There are several pieces of statuary scattered among the trees of the grove. One of them, a statue of Venus, is an exquisite conception, and so very pure that I wondered it should have found a place in a French garden. But not far from it there were two nude figures which were so shockingly sensual, and so clearly were intended by the sculptor to be so, that I turned away half indignant. Yet while I walked in the grove more than one French lady stopped leisurely to look at them through her glass.

When the weather is warm, the fashionable pedestrians flock to the trees of the Tuileries gardens, and among its cool recesses sit and talk the hours away. When the weather is colder and sunshine is desirable, the grounds immediately in front of the palace are more pleasant, as there the cold winds come not.

The Luxembourg gardens I have spoken of with some particularity in another place.

The *Jardin d'Hiver* is a winter garden, and contains many roofed hot-houses. The public are admitted by the payment of one franc. There are occasional displays of flowers and plants.

The *Champs Elysees* form one of the most delightful promenades in Paris. They contain no plants or flowers, but are so thickly planted with trees, that they may be called gardens. It was originally a promenade for Marie de Medici. It runs along the banks of the Seine, from the Place de la Concorde to the Triumphal Arch. The length is a mile and a quarter, the breadth three hundred and seventy-three yards. All the public fêtes take place on these fields. On the right is the promenade, and on the left under the trees and in open spaces are fairs, instrumental performances, shows, etc. etc. It is one of the most dazzling scenes in the night that ever eye beheld. I well remember that on my first visit to Paris, I wandered out of my hotel and saw the Champs Elysees in the evening. The sight was almost overpowering. The whole place was a scene of splendor. The trees and grounds were one blaze of lamps. Scattered over it were little theaters, concerts in the open air, every kind of show, coffee-houses, restaurants, and every kind of amusement. The concerts charge nothing. But if you enter within the ring you pay for a seat a trifle, and also for your refreshments. Almost every one who entered, (it was all in the open air,) bought a glass of something to drink, and sat down to enjoy it with the music. Fiddlers and mountebanks abounded in every direction, and beggars were more numerous if possible than the spectators. But not one *solicited* alms. It would jar too coarsely upon the Parisian refinement. A beggar sings, looks piteously, plays his flageolet or harp, but never *asks* for money! The whole scene presented to me was one of the most brilliant I ever witnessed, and it probably impressed me more from the fact that I was unprepared for it. I have often since frequented it in the evening, but never wearied of it.

The *Jardin des Plantes* is the most beautiful free garden in the world. It was founded in 1635 by Louis XIII. Buffon was its most celebrated superintendent. He devoted himself enthusiastically to its cultivation and development. It was at periods, during the revolutionary times, much neglected, but it continued to prosper through everything, unlike many of the other gardens. It consists of a botanical garden with several large hot-houses and green-houses attached; several galleries with scientific natural collections; a gallery of anatomy; a menagerie of living animals; a library of natural history; and lastly, a theater for public lectures. Everything is open to the people—lectures and all—and take it altogether, it is the finest and noblest garden in the world.

The *Jardin des Plantes* in the summer is one of the favorite resorts of Parisians, and although I frequented the spot, I never left it without a wonder that so much is thrown open free to the public. This is a remarkable feature of Paris and French institutions and public buildings. If possible, that which the people wish to see they can see for nothing. Painting-galleries, gardens, churches, and lectures are open to the crowd. This is in striking contrast with London. There nothing is free. The stranger pays to go over Westminster Abbey and St. Paul's. He cannot see anything without paying half a crown

JARDIN DES PLANTS.

for the sight. To *look* at a virgin or butler is worth at least a shilling.

The stranger usually enters the *Jardin des Plantes* by the eastern gate. The gallery of zoology is seen at the other end of the garden, while on either hand are beautiful avenues of lime trees. Beyond, on the right, is the menagerie, and on the left is a large collection of forest trees. Scattered all around in the open space, are beds containing all manner of medicinal and other plants from all parts of the earth. This part of the garden is to the botanist a very interesting spot. The flowering-shrubs are surrounded by a rail fence, and the level of the ground is sunk beneath that of other parts of the garden. There is a special "botanical garden," which is much frequented by students. On another avenue there are plantations of forest shrubs, and near them a café to accommodate visitors. Then stretching still further on, are new geological, mineralogical, and botanical galleries, all warmed in winter and summer, if necessary, by hot water, and capable of receiving the tallest tropical plants. Between the conservatories there are two beautiful mounds—one a labyrinth, and the other a collection of fir-trees. The labyrinth is one of the best and most beautiful I ever saw, far surpassing the celebrated one at Hampton court. Th mound is of a conical shape, and is completely covered by winding and intricate paths. The whole is surmounted by a splendid cedar of Lebanon. On the summit there are also seats covered with a bronze pavilion, and taking one of them the visitor can look over all the garden portions of Paris, and several of the villages near Paris. It is an exquisite view, and I know of no greater pleasure in the hot months than after walking over the garden to ascend the labyrinth and sit down in the cool shade of the pavilion, and watch the people wandering over the gardens, Paris, and the country. The western mound is a nursery of fir-trees, every known kind being collected there. There is another inclosure entered by a door at the foot of this mound, which in warm weather contains some of the most beautiful trees of New Holland, the Cape of Good Hope, Asia Minor, and the coast of Barbary. The ampitheater is here, also, where all the lectures are delivered. It will hold twelve hundred students but more than that number contrive to hear the lectures. In the enclosure there are twelve thousand different kinds of plants, and at the door stand two very beautiful Sicilian palms more than twenty-five feet in height.

The menagerie of the garden is one of the finest in the world, and is in some respects like the menagerie in London, though arranged with more taste. The cages are scattered over a large inclosure, and it seems like wandering over a forest and meeting the animals in their native wilds. After passing beneath the boughs of dark trees, it is startling to look up and see a Bengal tiger within a few feet of you, though he is caged, or to walk on further still, and confront a leopard. This part of the garden is a continual source of amusement to the younger portions of the community of Paris, to say nothing of the children of larger growth.

The cabinet of comparative anatomy is one of the finest parts of the garden, and we owe its excellence mainly to the great exertions of Cuvier. Every department is scientifically arranged, and the whole form, perhaps, the best collection of anatomical specimens in the world. In the first room are skeletons of the whale tribe, and many marine animals; in the next, are skeletons of the human species from every part of the globe. A suite of eleven rooms is taken up for the anatomy of birds, fishes, and reptiles. Several rooms are taken up with the exhibition of the muscles of all animals, including man. Others exhibit arms and legs; others still, brains and eyes, and the different organs of the body all arranged together, distinct from the remaining parts of the frame. In one room there is a singular collection of skulls of men from all countries, of all ages, and conditions. Celebrated murderers here are side by side with men of ancient renown.

The gallery of zoology is three hundred and ninety feet in length, and fronts the east end of the garden. The other galleries are all equally spacious and well arranged. The library is composed of works on natural history, and it is an unrivaled collection. It contains six thousand drawings, thirty thousand volumes, and fifteen thousand plants. This fine library is free on certain days to the world.

The good which results from such *free* exhibitions as that of the *Jardin des Plantes* is incalculable. The *people* become educated, enlightened to a degree they can never attain, upon the subjects illustrated, without them. This is one reason why Parisians are universally intelligent, even to the artisans. The poorer classes can scarcely help understanding botany, anatomy, zoology, and geology, with such a garden free of access. This is but a specimen of many like places in Paris. Lectures upon the sciences and arts are free to all who will hear, and whoever will may learn.

THE LUXEMBOURG PALACE AND GARDENS.

When France was governed by Louis Phillippe, the Palace Luxembourg was occupied by the Chamber of Peers, and it is now occupied by the Senate. It is a fine old building, and the impression it makes upon the stranger is an agreeable one. There is nothing in its history of particular interest, though its architecture is ancient.

I was better pleased with the Luxembourg gardens than with the palace. They are more beautiful than the Tuileries gardens and are much more democratic. Trees, plants, and flowers seemed to me to abound in them to a greater extent than in any other garden in Paris. On beautiful days they are full of women and children. Troops of the latter, beautiful as the sky which covers them, come to this place and play the long hours of a summer afternoon away, with their mothers and nurses following them about or sitting quietly under the shade of the trees, engaged in the double employment of knitting and watching the frolicsome humors of their children. I was very fond of going to these gardens in the afternoon, just to look at the array of mothers and children, and is was as pretty a sight as can be seen in all Paris. It is a sight which New York—be it spoken to her shame—does not furnish.

In the summer evenings a band of music plays for an hour to a vast multitude. Four of the finest bands in Paris take turns in playing at seven o'clock, four evenings in the week, and their music is of the highest order. Perhaps fifty thousand people are gathered at once, men, women, and children, to listen to the delicious music and

JARDIN ET PALAIS DU LUXEMBOURG.

the gathering in itself is a sight worth seeing. The great majority promenade slowly around the band, some stand still, and a very few rent chairs and sit. Nearly all the men smoke, and occasionally a woman does the same. But the flavor of the tobacco is execrable. What substitute the French use I know not, but the villainous smells which come from the cigars smoked by the majority of Frenchmen indicate something very bad. Cabbage leaves—so extensively used to make cigars with in England—do not give forth so vile a stench.

I always noticed in the Luxembourg gardens many fine looking men, and some elegantly dressed and lady-like women, but the majority of the latter were grisettes, or mistresses. Many students were promenading with their little temporary wives, not in the least ashamed to make such a public display of their vices. The women present might be divided into four classes; the gay but not vicious, students' mistresses, ordinary strumpets, and the poor but virtuous, by far the majority belonging to those classes which have a poor reputation. Yet the conduct of those women was in every respect proper. There were no indecent gestures, and not a loud word spoken which would have been out of place in a drawing-room. Not a woman addressed one of the opposite sex.

Directly in front of the Luxembourg palace there is a bower of orange trees and statues railed off from other portions of the garden. It presents an extremely beautiful appearance. In front of it there is a fine basin of water and a fountain. Four nude marble boys support a central basin, from which the water pours. The ground directly in front of the palace is lower than it is on either side, and a row of fine orange trees extends out on either hand from the palace, and flowers of every description mingle their fragrance with that of the orange blossoms. Groves of trees extend far to the right and left, and to the south, there are fine gardens devoted to the cultivation of rare plants and every variety of fruit trees.

The best thing I know about the Luxembourg palace is, that it has a gallery of paintings. It formerly was used to exhibit paintings by the old masters, but now nothing is allowed a place in the Luxembourg gallery but pictures of living artists. As soon as the artist dies, his pictures which hang in the Luxembourg, and which have been purchased by the government, are at once removed to the Louvre, where only paintings of men now dead are on exhibition.

The collection in the Luxembourg is in many respects a a very fine one, but it has the fault of all the modern French and continental pictures—there is too much sensuality exhibited upon the canvas. The school is too voluptuous—too licentious. I can put up with anything not positively indecent for the sake of art, but I cannot put up with French pictures. Their nakedness is too disgusting, for it is not relieved by sentiment, unless of the basest kind. This remark of course does not apply to all the pictures I saw. Some of them are very fine, especially those of Delaroche and the war pictures of Horace Vernet. Near the entrance there is a beautiful group by Delaistre, representing Cupid and Psyche.

One of the pictures in this gallery haunts me still. It is an illustration of one of Dante's immortal verses—his visit to the lake of Brimstone. The poet with a wreath of laurel round his brow stands in the center of a little boat, while his conductor in the stream propels the craft with one oar over the boiling and surging sea of hell His countenance is filled with mingled astonishment and horror, yet he preserves his wits and observes very critically all that is about him. One poor wretch lifts his head from the liquid fire, and fastens his jaws upon the rim of the boat in his terrible agony, while one of the attendants of the boat with an oar endeavors to beat him back. On the other side a ghostly wretch has fastened his long teeth into a fellow-sufferer. The shades of light and darkness are so mingled that the effect is very striking. It is the most horrible picture I ever looked at, and I would much rather sleep in Madame Tassaud's chamber of horrors, than look at it again. In the next apartment there is a picture of Christ, which struck me as the best I ever looked at. The divine sweetness of the human and the grandeur of the God were united with wonderful skill. The face was half-sorrowful, as if the heart were filled with thoughts of a sinful, suffering world, and still upon the brow the very sunshine of heaven rested. The impression which that face made upon me will never be entirely obliterated, and its effect was far different from the illustration of Dante. The two pictures, it seemed to me, teach a useful lesson. It is that men are to be saved through love, and not through fear. Let men see God's beauty and loveliness, and you will more surely win them from error than by showing them the horrors of hell.

The origin of the Luxembourg palace was as follows: about the middle of the sixteenth century, one Robert de Harley erected a large house in the middle of the gardens. In 1583 the house was bought and enlarged by the duke of Luxembourg, and in 1612 Marie de Medicis bought it for ninety thousand francs, and then commenced the present palace. During the first year of the revolution it was used for a prison; then for an assembly-room for the consuls; still later as the chamber for the peers and now the French senate meet in it. It contains a large library, but the people cannot have access to its well-stored shelves. Students can, however, by making proper application, consult the library.

One evening while walking in the Luxembourg gardens, the band playing exquisite music, and the crowd promenading to it, I met a friend, an American, who has resided in Paris for seventeen years. Taking his arm we fell into the current of people, and soon met a couple of quite pretty looking ladies arm-in-arm. They were dressed exactly alike and their looks were very much of the same pattern, and as to their figures, I certainly could not tell one from the other with their faces turned away.

"They are sisters," said my friend, "and you will scarcely believe me when I tell you that I saw them in this very garden ten years ago." I replied that I could hardly credit his story, for the couple still looked young, and I could hardly think that so many years ago they would have been allowed by their anxious mamma to promenade in such a place. I told my friend so, and a smile overspread his countenance. He then told me their history. Ten years ago and they were both shop-girls, very pretty and very fond of the attentions of young men. As shop-girls, they occasionally found time to come and hear the music in the gardens of an evening, and cast glances at the young students. Soon they were student's mistresses. Their paramours were generous and wealthy young men, and they fared well. For four years they were as faithful, affectionate, and devoted to the young men as any wives in all France. They indulged in no gallantries or light conduct with other men, and among the students were reckoned as fine specimens of the class. Four happy years passed away, when one morning the poor girls awoke to a sad change. The collegiate course was through, and the young collegians were going back to their fathers' mansions in the provinces. Of course the grisettes could not be taken with them, and the ties of years were suddenly and rudely to be snapped asunder. At first they were frantic in their grief. When they entered upon their peculiar relations with the students, they well knew that this must be the final consummation, but then it looked a great way off. That they really loved the young men, no one can doubt. It would not be strange for a little shop-girl to even adore a talented university student, however insignificant he might be to other people. To her he is everything that is great and noble. These girls knew well that they were not wives, but mistresses, yet when the day of separation came, it was like parting husband and wife. But there was no use in struggling with fate, and they consoled themselves by transferring their affections to two more students. Again after a term of years they were forsaken, until the flower of their youth was gone, and no one desired to support them as mistresses. Then a downward step was taken. Nothing but promiscuous prostitution was before them—except starvation. And still they could not forget their old life, and came nightly to this public promenade to see the old sights, and possibly with the hope of drawing some unsophisticated youth into their net. While my friend repeated their story, the couple frequently passed us, and I could hardly believe that persons whose deportment was so modest and correct, could be what he had designated them; but as the twilight deepened, and we were walking away, I noticed that they were no longer together, and one had the arm of a man, and was walking, like us, away from the gardens.

I do not know as I could give the reader a better idea of a great class of women in Paris, than by relating the brief history of these girls, and certainly I could not sketch a sadder picture. To the stranger the social system of France may seem very pleasant and gay, but it is in reality a sorrowful one. While the mistress is young, she has a kind of happiness, but when she loses her beauty, then her wretchedness begins. But I will dwell upon this whole subject more fully in another place.

THE GOBELINS.

One of the interesting places which I visited in Paris, is the famous Tapestry and Carpet Manufactory in the Rue Mouffetard. The walk is quite a long one from the Garden of Plants, but the wonders of art and industry which are shown to the visiter, amply repay for the trouble and toil in getting to the manufactory.

I first passed through several rooms, upon the walls of which were hung some of the finest of the tapestries which are finished. I was astonished to see the perfection to which the art is carried. Some of the tapestries, were quite as beautiful as some of the paintings in the Louvre. Each piece was a picture of some spot, scene, or character, and the workmanship is of such an exquisite kind, that it is extremely difficult to believe that real paintings of the highest order are not before you. Yet all the shades and expressions are wrought into the web, by the hands of the skillful workmen. I visited six of the work-rooms, where the men were manufacturing the tapestries. It was a wonderful sight. The workman stands immediately behind the web, and a basket containing woolen yarn, or a thread of every variety or color, is at his feet. The design, usually an exquisite picture, stands behind him in a good light. A drawing of the part of the landscape or figure first to be made is sketched by pencil upon the web, and with the picture to be copied constantly in sight, the workman or artist, as he should be called, works slowly upon his task, glad if in a day he can work into the tapestry a branch, a hand, or an eye. In some of the work-rooms, the finest tapestries were being manufactured, and in others only very fine rugs and carpets.

In 1450 a man by the name of Jean Gobelin acquired considerable property in the region of Rue Mouffetard by dyeing and making carpets. His sons carried on the business in his name, and the manufactory was celebrated; hence the name, Gobelins. Louis XIV. erected it into a royal manufactory, and it has continued such ever since. Between one and two hundred men are constantly in the employ of the government, in the manufactory, and as men of great skill and refined tastes are required, a good rate of wages is paid. The workmen seemed to be very intelligent, and were dressed, many of them, at least, like gentlemen. The tapestries, carpets, &c. &c., which are manufactured at this place, are intended for the emperor, the palaces, and for other monarchs to whom they may be presented in the name of the French emperors. They are the finest specimens of their kind in the world. There is another manufactory connected with the Gobelins, for dyeing wools, and they are dyed better than in any other place, or at least none can be purchased elsewhere so fitted for the wants of the tapestry workers. There is also a school of design connected with it, and a course of lectures is delivered by able and accomplished men.

The carpet manufactory is one of the best, and perhaps *the* best, in the world. The Parisian carpets are not equal to those manufactured here. It often takes five and ten years to make a carpet, and the cost is as high sometimes as thirty thousand dollars. None are ever sold. One was one made for the Louvre gallery, consisting of seventy-two pieces, and being over thirteen hundred feet in length.

I have never been more astonished with any exhibition of the fruits of industry and art, than with the carpets and tapestries in the Rue Mouffetard. Some of the latter excel in beauty the best pictures in Europe, and when one reflects that each tint is of wool, worked into the web by the careful fingers of the workman, that every line, every muscle, is wrought as distinctly and beautifully as upon canvas, it excites admiration and wonder. The rooms are open for four hours two days in the week, and they were crowded when I was there, and principally by foreigners.

On my way back, I stopped in the Garden of Plants, and seated myself upon the benches beneath the shade of the trees. After resting awhile, I entered a restaurant and ordered dinner, as I could scarcely wait to return to the hotel, and in Paris, where a bargain is made at so much per day for hotel charges, including meals, if one is absent at dinner the proper sum is deducted from the daily charges.

I did not succeed in getting a good dinner for a fair price, which I always could do at the hotel. It was so poor that a little while after, I tried a cup of coffee and a roll upon the *Champs Elysees*, which were delicious enough to make up for the poor dinner.

In front of me there was an orchestre, and some singers, who discoursed very good music for the benefit of all persons who patronized the restaurant. A multitude of ladies and gentlemen were ranged under the trees before them, sipping coffee, wine, or brandy. The sight was a very gay one, but not uncommon in Paris.

I went one day outside the walls of Paris, and took dinner in a beautiful spot where the sun was almost entirely excluded by the trees and shrubs, in gardens attached to a restaurant. I had a capital dinner, too, for a small price, better than I could have had for double the money at a London hotel.

CHAPTER VIII.

THE PEOPLE—CLIMATE—PUBLIC INSTITUTIONS—HOTEL DES INVALIDES.

THE PEOPLE.

THE French people, so far as one may judge from Paris, are very difficult to study and understand. They are easy of access, but it is difficult to account for the many and strange anomalies in their character.

The intense love of gayety and the amount of elegant trifling which shows itself everywhere as a national characteristic, does not prepare one to believe that some of the greatest of mathematicians, philosophers, and scientific men are Frenchmen and Parisians; but such is the fact. The French are fickle, love pleasure, and one would think that these qualities would unfit men for coolness, perseverance, and prolonged research; and I am sometimes inclined to think that the proficiency of the French in philosophy, the arts, and sciences, is not so much the result of patient investigation and laborious and continued study, as a kind of intuition which amounts to genius. The French mind is quick, and does not plod slowly toward eminence; it leaps to it. Certainly, in brilliancy of talents the French surpass every other nation. I will not do them the injustice to speak of them as they are at this moment—crushed under the despotism of Louis Napoleon—but as they have been in the last few years, and indeed for centuries. Paris is a city of brilliant men and women. A French orator is one of the most eloquent speakers, one of the most impressive men, any country can furnish. The intelligence of the Paris artisans would surprise many people in America. We have only to examine the journals which before the advent of the empire were almost exclusively taken by the working-classes of Paris, to see the proof of this. Their leaders were written in the best essay-style, and were the result of careful thought and application. Such journals could never have gained a fair support from the artisans of New York. They were not mere news journals, nor filled up with ove-stories. They contained articles of great worth, which required on the part of the reader a love of abstract truth and the consideration of it. Such journals sold by thousands in Paris before Napoleon III. throttled the newspapers. These very men were fond of pleasure and pursued it, and I have been told by residents, that often persons of a foppish exterior and fashionable conduct, are also celebrated for the extent of their learning. At home we rarely look for talent or learning among the devotees of fashion, or at least, among those who exalt fashion above all moral attributes.

It seems to me that the French are more gifted by nature than the English. The English mind is more sluggish, but in all that is practical, it gains the goal of success, while the French mind often fails of it. In theory, the French have always had the most delightful of republics—in fact, a wretched despotism. So, too, they have had an idea of liberty, such as is seldom understood even in America, but real liberty has existed rarely in France.

The laboring men of Paris perhaps never saw the inside of a school-room, but they are educated. They know how to read, and through the newspapers, the library, the popular lecture and exhibition, they have gained what many who spend most of their earlier years in school never gain. From an experience which justifies it, I be lieve the soberest part of Paris is its class of artisans. They may possess many wrong and foolish opinions, but they are a noble class of men. They are a majority of them republicans, and though they consent to the inevitable necessity—obedience to the monarch and endurance of a monarchy—yet they indulge in hopes of a brilliant future for France. They know very well how their rights are trampled upon, and feel keenly what a disgraceful condition Paris and all France occupies at the present time, but are by no means satisfied with it. They well know that there is no real liberty in Paris to-day; that no journal dares to speak the whole truth for fear of losing its existence; and that the noblest men of the republic are in exile. The trouble is, that the lower classes of the provinces are grossly ignorant, and do not desire a republic, nor care for liberty. Thus, those who are intelligent and have aspirations after freedom, are borne down by the ignorant.

One of the characteristics of the people of Paris, for which they are known the world over, is their politeness. I noticed this in all circles and in all places. In England John Bull stares at your dress if it differs from his own, and hunts you to the wall. Or if anything in your speech or manners pleases him, he laughs in your face. But in Paris, the Frenchman never is guilty of so ill-bred an action as to laugh at anybody in his presence, however provoking the occasion. If you are lost and inquire the way, he will run half a mile to show you, and will not even hear of thanks. I remember once in Liverpool asking in a barber's-shop the way to the Waterloo hotel. A person present, who was so well-dressed that I supposed him a gentleman, said that he was going that way and would show me. I replied that I could find the spot, the street having been pointed out by the barber. The "gentleman" persisted in accompanying me. When we reached the hotel I thanked him, but he was not to be shaken off. He raised his hat and said, "I hope I may have the happiness of drinking wine with you!" I was angry at such meanness, and I gave him a decided negative. "But," he persisted, "you will drink ale with me?" I replied, "I never drink ale." "But," said he, "you will give *me* a glass?" This persistence was so disgusting that I told the man I would give him in charge of the police as an impostor if he did not leave, which he did at this hint, instantly.

The only time that I ever experienced anything but politeness in Paris, was when in a great hurry I chanced to hit a workman with a basket upon his head. The concussion was so great that the basket was dashed to the pavement. He turned round very slowly, and with a grin upon his countenance said, "Thank you, sir!" This was politeness with a little too much sarcasm. It was spoken so finely that I burst into a laugh, and the Frenchman joined me in it.

The shop-keepers of Paris are a very polite class, and are as avaricious as they are polite. The habit which they have of asking a higher price than they expect to get is a bad one. It is a notorious fact that foreigners in Paris can rarely buy an article so cheaply as a native. There are always quantities of verdant Englishmen visiting Paris, and the temptation to cheat them is too great to be resisted by the wide-awake shop-keepers. Besides, it satisfies a grudge they all have against Englishmen. I always found it an excellent way not to buy until the shop-keeper had lowered his price considerably. Sometimes I would state my country, and the saleswoman would roguishly pretend that for that reason she reduced the price. I remember stopping once in the Palais Royal to gaze at some pretty chains in the window. A black-eyed little woman came to the door, and I asked the price of a ring which struck my fancy. She gave it, and I shook my head, telling her that in the country which I came from I could get such a ring for less money. She wanted to know the name of my country, and when I told her it was America, she said in a charming manner, "Oh! you come from the grand republic! you shall have the ring for so many francs," naming a sum far less than she had at first asked. Of course, I did not suppose she sacrificed a *sou* for the sake of my country, but it showed how apt are the Paris shop-keepers at making excuses. An Englishman or American would have solemnly declared he would not take a penny less—and then very coolly give the lie to his assertion; at any rate, I have seen English and American tradesman do so.

A majority of the shop-keepers of Paris are women, and many of them young and pretty. I certainly have seen more beauty of face in the shops than on the Boulevards of Paris. Young girls from the ages of fifteen to twenty-five, are usually the clerks in all the shops, which are often presided over by a grown-up woman who is mistress of the establishment, her husband being by no means the first man in the establishment, but rather a silent partner.

The grisettes are often girls of industry and great good-nature, but the morals of the class are lamentably low. They are easily seduced from the path of right, and are led to form temporary alliances with men, very often the students of the Latin Quarter. They rarely degrade themselves for money or for such considerations, but it is for love or pleasure that they fall. They are given to adventures and intrigues, until they become the steady paramours of men, and then they are true and constant. Often they are kept and regarded more like wives than mistresses. I should not do entire justice to this class if I were to convey the idea that all of them are thus debauched. Many marry poor young men, but such is not usually the case; a poor young man seeks a wife with a small dowry. They have little hope of wedded life—it will never offer itself to them. Their shop-life is dreary, monotonous, and sometimes exacting. If they will desert it, pleasure presents an enticing picture; a life of idleness, dancing, and a round of amusements.

I was very much struck by a remark made to me by one of the purest men in France—that a Frenchman is more apt to be jealous of his mistress than his wife, and that as a general rule, a mistress is more true to her lover than a wife is to her husband. This is horrible, yet to a certain extent I am convinced it is true. And it may be so, and women be no more to blame in the matter than the other sex. To-day, in the fashionable society of our great cities, how much does it injure a wealthy young man's prospects for matrimony, if it is a well-known fact that he is a libertine? And how long can such a state of things continue without dragging down the women who marry such men? If a lady cares not if her lover is a libertine, she cannot possess much of genuine virtue. The fashionable men of Paris keep mistresses—so do those of all classes, the students, perhaps, according to their numbers, being worse in this respect than all others.

It is not strange, such being the case, that the women are frail.

One thing is specially noticeable among the ladies of Paris—the care with which they are guarded before marriage, and the freedom of their conduct after. In countries where there is almost universal virtue among women, the faith in them is strong, and a freedom of intercourse between the sexes is allowed previous to marriage, which is never tolerated in such a place as Paris. In New England it is not thought improper for a young gentleman and lady to enjoy a walk together in the country, and alone, but in France it would ruin the reputation of a woman. A friend of mine in London warmly invited a young friend of his in Paris to come over and make his family a visit on some special occasion. The Parisian wrote back that he should like nothing better than such a trip, but that business would not allow of it. "Then," wrote back my friend, "let your sister come." The reply was decided: "Oh, no! it would never do for the young lady to make such a trip alone, for the sake of her reputation." It would have struck this Frenchman as a very singular fact, if he had known that in America a young lady will travel thousands of miles alone, without the slightest harm to her reputation.

But when the French woman *marries*, the tables are turned. Then she possesses a freedom such as no American lady, thank heaven, wishes to enjoy. She may have half a dozen open lovers, and society holds its tongue. Her husband probably has as many mistresses. It is not considered improper in Paris either for a husband and father to love his mistress, or a wife and mother to love her acknowledged lover, and that man not her husband. The intrigues which are carried on by married people in

Paris, would shock sober people in America, or at least, outside our largest and wickedest cities.

The social state of France is exceedingly bad, and when American religious writers profess to be shocked at the theories of the French Socialists, I am inclined to ask them what they think of the *actual condition* of the French people. Some of the Socialists have been driven to extremes, because Paris has no conception of the home and the family. The enemies of Socialism in France are, in practice, worse than their enemies in theory. Who is the man now ruling France? Does the world not know him to have long been an open and thoroughly debauched libertine? The same is true of other distinguished friends of "law and order."

The outward condition of the streets of Paris often deceives the stranger as to the morality of the city. Said one gentleman to me, who had spent several weeks at a fashionable Paris hotel, "Paris is one of the quietest, pleasantest towns in the world, and as for its morals, I can see nothing which justifies its bad reputation abroad." After a week's stay in it, such was my own opinion. Things which are tolerated in London and New York streets, are not permitted in the streets of Paris. A street-walker ventured to accost an Englishman in Paris at night, and was taken in charge by the police. But this outward fairness only indicates that in Paris, even the vices are regulated by the state. Bad women cannot make a display and accost men in the street, but they abound, and what is far worse, in all the circles and gradations of society. It is society which is corrupt there. One need but to look at the morals of its great men, to see this at once. What is the moral character of the first men in the empire? Bad, as no Frenchman will deny.

Some of the very men who have won in America golden opinions for their noble and eloquent advocacy of liberty, have been in their private lives devoid of all virtue. It only shows the social condition of the country. Some writers deny these allegations against Paris, but no man will who has lived in it, and is honest and candid. Paris abounds with illegitimate children. The statistics tell the story. Ten thousand illegitimate children are born every year in that city! What can be the morality of any town, while such facts exist in reference to its condition?

I hate all cant, but am satisfied that the chief reason why France does not succeed better in her revolutions is, because she lacks the steadiness which a sincere devotion to religion gives to a nation. The country needs less man-worship and more God-worship. It needs less adulation of beautiful women, and more real appreciation of true womanhood.

There is a great deal of art-worship in Paris, but it does not seem to really elevate the condition of the people. The pictures and the statues are generally of the most sensuous kind. Do these things improve the morals of a city or nation? If so, why is it that wherever naked pictures and sensual statuary abound, the people are licentious and depraved? In America such things are not tolerated by the mass of the people, and there prevails a higher style of virtue than in any other land. But in France and in Italy, the beauty of the human form upon canvas or in marble, in however offensive a manner, is adored—and in those countries the people have little morality.

The French *home* is not the home of England or America. The genuine Parisian lives on the street, or in the theater or ball-room. He never lives at home.

Hence, the mothers and daughters of England and America are not there to be found. "Comparisons are odious," but I cannot express my meaning so plainly without making them, and I state but the simple truth. Young men and women are not taught to seek their pleasure at the family fireside, but beyond it, and a man marries not to make a home, but to make money or a position in society. Women, too, often marry simply to attain liberty of action.

Another characteristic of the French, and especially of Parisians, is that they educate their sons to no such independence as is everywhere common in America. The young Parisian is dependent upon his father—he cannot support himself; and men of thirty and forty, who are helpless, are to be seen in all classes throughout the great cities of France.

Whether there is just ground for expecting that France will very soon throw off the despotism which now weighs her down, I am incompetent, perhaps, to judge; but I fear not. There is a very noble class of men in Paris—I know this by experience—who hate all despotism and love freedom, but I fear they will for centuries be overcome by ignorance and the love of pleasure, on the part of the people, and knavery and brute force on the part of rulers.

CLIMATE—POPULATION—POLICE, ETC.

The weather of Paris during the summer months is warm and usually delightful, but in winter it is very cold —much colder than it is in London. But Paris escapes the horrible fogs which envelop London in November and December. The weather, too, though cold, is wholesome and often conducive to health. The two months of fog in London are often termed the suicidal months, because of the number of persons who destroy their own lives in those months. The people of Paris with their mercurial temperaments would never endure it for a long time, at least.

Fuel is exceedingly dear in Paris, and the buildings are not made for in-door comfort. If they were as warmly made as the houses of New York, they would be comfortable in winter, but such not being the case, and fuel being costly, comfort in private apartments is rarely to be had by any but the rich. Coal is not used to any great extent, though charcoal is burned in small quantities, but wood is the fuel principally used. It is sold in small packages, and is principally brought up from the distant provinces by the canals. The amount of wood required to make what a Frenchman would call a glowing fire, would astonish an American. A half a dozen sticks, not much larger or longer than his fingers, laid crosswise in a little hearth, is sufficient for a man's chamber. A log which one of our western farmers would think nothing of consuming in a winter's evening, would bring quite a handsome sum in Paris on any winter day. The truth is, the economical traveler had better not spend his winter in

Paris, for comfort at that time costs money. The houses admit such volumes of cold air, the windows are so loose and the doors such wretched contrivances, and that, too, in the best of French cities, that the stranger sighs for the comforts of home. Nowhere in the world is so much taste displayed as in Paris, in the furnishing of apartments. This is known as far as Paris is, but it is always the *outside appearance* which is attended to, and nothing more. It is like the Parisian dandy who wears a fine coat, hat, and false bosom, but has no shirt. The homes of Paris are got up, many of them at least, upon this principle. The rooms are elegantly furnished, and in pleasant weather are indeed very pleasant to abide in, but let a cold day come, and they are as uncomfortable as can be, and the ten thousand conveniencies which a New York or London household would think it impossible to be without, are wanting.

The longest day in Paris is sixteen hours, the shortest eight. The cities of Europe are distant from it as follows: Brussels, one hundred and eighty-nine miles; Berlin, five hundred and ninety-three; Frankfort, three hundred and thirty-nine; Lisbon, one thousand one hundred and four; Rome, nine hundred and twenty-five; Madrid, seven hundred and seventy-five; Constantinople, one thousand five hundred and seventy-four; St. Petersburgh, one thousand four hundred and five. These places are all easily reached from Paris in these modern days of railways and steamers.

The situation of Paris is much more favorable to health than that of London. London is a low plain—Paris is upon higher ground; yet London is the healthiest city. The reason is, that the latter is so thoroughly drained, and the tide of the Thames sweeping through it twice a day, carries away all the impurities of the sewers. Paris might surpass London in its sewerage easily, but as it is, some of its narrow streets in warm weather are fairly insupportable, from the intolerable stench arising in them.

The population of Paris is considerably more than a million. The number of births in a year is a little more than thirty thousand, and of these, ten thousand are illegitimate. This fact speaks volumes in reference to the morals of Paris. The deaths usually fall short of the births by about four thousand. The increase of population in France is great, though it is now a very populous country.

The increase in forty years is more than nine millions. The births in France in one year are about eight hundred and ninety-seven thousand, and the deaths eight hundred and sixty-five thousand. Of the births, more than seventy thousand are illegitimate. This fact shows that the morals of Paris, in one respect, are worse than those of the provinces.

It is calculated that one-half of the inhabitants of Paris are *working* men; the rest are men who live by some trade or profession, or have property and live upon it. Paris has more than eighty thousand servants, and at least seventy thousand paupers. The latter class, as a matter of course, varies with the character of the times; sometimes, a bad season enlarging the number by many thousands. There is an average population of fifteen thousand in the hospitals; five thousand in the jails; and at least, twenty thousand foundlings are constantly supported in the city. The annual number of suicides in France is nearly six thousand. Yet the French are a very gay people!

The police regulations of Paris are very good, but not

so good as those of London, though New York might learn from her many useful lessons. Rogues thrive better in Paris than in London. The Paris policeman wears no distinctive dress, and there are streets in which if you are attacked by night, your cries will call no officer to the rescue. The police have been proved often to be in league with bad men and bad women, and these cases are occurring from day to day. I should not like to walk alone on a winter's night, after midnight, anywhere for half a mile on the southern side of the Seine. Some of the streets are exceedingly narrow, and are tenanted by strange people. Still, one might have many curious adventures in them, and escape safely—but *La Morgue* tells a mysterious tale every day of some dark deed—a suicide or a murder, perhaps.

Getting lost after midnight in one of the narrow streets of Paris, is not particularly pleasant, especially if every person you meet looks like a thief. The police system of Paris is in one respect far more strict than that of London—in political matters. Every stranger, or native, suspected in the least of tendencies to republicanism, is continually watched and dogged wherever he moves. While in Paris, my whereabouts was constantly known to the police, and though I made several changes in my abode, I was followed each time, and my address taken; yet I was but an inoffensive republican from America. A man must be careful to whom he talks of French despots, or despotism. For speaking against Louis Napoleon in an omnibus, a Frenchman was sentenced to two years imprisonment, and men have been exiled for a less offense The police are everywhere to detect conspiracy or radicalism, but are more slack in reference to the safety of people in the streets.

One pleasant feature of Paris is its great number of baths, public and private. The artisan who has little money to spare can go to the Seine any day, and for six cents take a bath under a large net roofing. A gentleman, to be sure, would hardly like to try such a place, but the working people are not particular. It is cheap, and in the hot weather it is a great luxury to bathe, to say nothing of the necessity of the thing. To take a bath in a first-rate French hotel is quite another matter. Every luxury will be afforded, and the price will be quite as high as the bath is luxurious.

Pleasure trips are getting to be quite common in France, in imitation of the English, on a majority of the railways. The fares for these pleasure trips are very much reduced. I noticed the walls one day covered with advertisements of a pleasure trip to Havre and back for only seven francs. The second and third class carriages on the French railroads are quite comfortable, but the first are very luxurious. Trains run from Paris to all parts of the country, at almost all hours of the day and night.

PUBLIC INSTITUTIONS.

There is no city in the world so blessed with educational institutions of the first class as Paris, and no government fosters the arts and sciences to such an extent as the French government, whether under the administration of king, president, or emperor. The government constantly rewards discoveries, holds out prizes to students and men of genius. The educational colleges are without number, and the lectures are free. There is one compliment which the stranger is forced to pay the French government—it encourages a republicanism among men of genius in learning, the arts and sciences, if it does put its heel upon the slighest tendency toward political republicanism.

And not Paris, or France alone, reaps the advantage of this liberality—the whole civilized world does the same. Go into the university region, and you will always see great numbers of foreigners who have come to take advantage of the public institutions of Paris. The English go there to study certain branches of medicine, which are more skillfully treated in the French medical schools than anywhere else in the world. Many young Americans are in Paris, at the present time, studying physic or law.

The difference between the cost of education in England and France is great. Three hundred dollars a year would carry a French student in good style through the best French universities. To go through an English college five times that sum would be necessary.

Palais de l'Institut.

The *Institut de France* lies upon the southern branch of the Seine, just opposite the Louvre, which is north of the river. The *Institute* is divided into five academies, and the funds which support the institution are managed by a committee of ten members, two from an academy, and the minister of public instruction, who presides over the committee. The academies are—first the *Academie Francaise;* second, the *Académie Royale des Inscriptions et Belle-Lettres;* third, the *Académie Royale des Sciences;* fourth, the *Académie Royale des Beaux Arts;* and fifth, the *Académie Royale des Sciences Morales et Politiques.* Members of one academy are eligible to the other four, and each receives a salary of three hundred dollars. The Institute has a library common to the five academies, the whole number of members amounting to two hundred and seventeen. If a member does not attend the proceedings and discussions, and cannot give a good reason for his absence, he is liable to expulsion.

The *Académie Francaise* consists of forty members, who are devoted to the composition of the dictionary and the purification of the French language. An annual prize is awarded of two thousand francs for poetry, a prize of ten thousand francs for the best work of French history and fifteen hundred francs is given every other year to some deserving but poor student, for his attainments.

The Belle-Lettres Academy is composed of forty members, and ten free academicians—the latter receive no salary. It has many foreign associates or honorary members. Its members pursue the study of the learned languages, antiquities, etc. etc. A yearly prize of ten thousand francs is awarded by it for memoirs, and another for medals.

The Academy of Sciences has sixty-five members, beside ten free academicians. It is divided into eleven sections, as follows: six members are devoted to geometry, six to mechanics, six to astronomy, six to geography and navigation, three to general philosophy, six to chemistry, six to minerology, six to botany, six to rural economy and the veterinary art, six to anatomy and geology, six to medicine and surgery. Prizes are awarded by this academy, yearly, for physical sciences, statistics, physiology, mechanics, improvements in surgery and medicine; for improvements in the art of treating patients, for rendering any art or trade less insalubrious, for discoveries, for mathematical studies, and also a prize to the best scholar in the Polytechnic school.

The Academy of Fine Arts has forty members, who are divided into five sections—painting, sculpture, architecture, engraving, and musical composition. It awards prizes to the best students in the arts, and sends to the French Academy at Rome, free of all expense, the successful students, who are educated at the expense of the state.

The Academy of *Sciences Morales et Politiques* has thirty members, divided into the following sections: philosophy, moral philosophy, legislation, jurisprudence, political economy, history, and the philosophy of history.

The building of the Institute is surmounted by a splendid dome, and it presents a striking appearance to th stranger. It immediately fronts the foot-bridge which crosses the Seine to the Louvre.

The university of France it is supposed was founded by Charlemagne. It is a magnifiçent and truly liberal institution, and is under the authority of the minister of public instruction. It has five departments, an immense library and funds for aged or infirm teachers.

The Academy of Paris consists of five faculties—science letters, theology, law, and medicine. In the department of sciences, which includes that of mathematical astronomy, Leverrier occupies a professor's chair—the man who demonstrated the existence of another planet by mathematical calculations, and pointed out the place where it must be found.

The Faculty of Law has seventeen professors. Four years of study are necessary to gain the highest honors, or the title of *Docteur en droit.*

The Faculty of Medicine has twenty-six professorships, with salaries varying from two thousand to ten thousand francs a year. Every student before taking his degree must serve the government one year, at least, in a hospital. This is an admirable regulation. The lectures are all gratuitous, and what is better still, they are open to the people and the world. Any foreigner can attend the course of lectures of the most celebrated men in France, and indeed in the world, for nothing. The law students number about three thousand; those studying medicine about three thousand; and those studying the sciences about fifteen hundred. Foreign students are admitted upon the same terms as French, and a diploma given by an American college, if it be of high repute, will put the student upon the same footing as a French *bachelier et lettres* when the object is to study law or medicine.

The College Royal has twenty-eight professors, who give gratuitous lectures on astronomy, mathematics, philosophy, medicine, chemistry, natural history, law, ethics, etc. etc. There is a college of Natural History, connected with the *Jardin des Plantes*, with fifteen professors. The *Ecole Normale* is an institution for the education of students who intend to become candidates for professorships. There are in Paris besides these, five royal colleges where a student is boarded as well as educated. The charge for board is two hundred dollars a year; the additional charges, educational and otherwise, are only twenty dollars, which the published terms state, "*does not include music or dancing!*"

Among the literary and scientific societies is the *Institut Historique*, where public and gratuitous lectures are given. A journal is published, and all that members pay for it, and the advantages of the institution, is about four dollars a year. There is a flourishing agricultural society, a society for the encouragement of national industry, one for the improvement of national horticulture, one for the civilization and colonization of Africa, one for the promotion of commercial knowledge, etc. etc.

Besides the many colleges to which I have barely alluded, and the societies, there are twenty or thirty literary and scientific societies of note in Paris.

It will not be necessary to be more particular to convince the reader that no other city in the world has the educational advantages of Paris. What a privilege it must be to a poor Parisian to live near such schools and colleges, we can at once perceive. If a young man has talents or genius, his poverty need be no bar to his advancement. He is taken up at once. He is not the charity student of America, for the very fact that without money and friends he has by sheer force of native genius made his way into the places given only to students poor and talented, adds to his fame, and he is quite as well if not better liked for it. What an advantage the many kinds of lectures, which are given to all who please to attend gratuitously, must be to all inquiring minds in Paris, we can feel at once. The artisan if he can spare an hour can listen to one of the most brilliant lectures upon history, either of the sciences, or medicine, side by side with the young aristocrat. Nothing higher in character is to be had in Paris or out of it than that which he listens to without cost. The effect of this vast system of public instruction is very great, and the influence of the colleges and learned societies upon society is wonderful. There is no spirit of exclusiveness, such as characterizes the English and some of the American colleges, and the people are not prejudiced against them. This system of instruction is almost perfect, *of its kind*, but France lacks one thing which America has—a system of common schools, which shall educate *the children.* Far better have this system and lack the one she has now, but if she only had our common school system together with her colleges and academies, she would surpass, by far, any other nation. America very much needs such a system. It is free, broad, and liberal, and with ordinary care will make any country glorious in the sciences and arts. Certainly until America cares less for mere cash and more for the arts and sciences, until she is generous enough to foster them and appropriate money to help young men of genius, and offer prizes to men of talent, the fine arts will not prosper with us. Only the arts which in a pecuniary sense *pay*, will thrive, and the rest will live a starveling life. Can we rest content with such a prospect? No country is better able to be generous in such matters than America.

While in Paris I made the acquaintance of several students of law and medicine from America, and from them I learned that the professors in all the different institutions are exceedingly polite and kind to foreign students, and especially to Americans. Foreign diplomas are granted by the different colleges, and no difference is made between a native and a foreign scholar.

The students of Paris are an intellectual class, and as a

body are inclined at all times to be democratic. In England and in America learning seems always to incline to conservatism. The great schools and colleges are opposed to radicalism. This is generally true in America, in the old institutions of learning, and it is emphatically true of England. Cambridge and Oxford are the strong-holds of the blindest toryism. They are two hundred years behind the age. But in Paris this is not the case. The colleges are reformatory and radical. The Academies have the same disposition, only it is modified. Many of the members of the French academy are sincere republicans. I cannot account for this singular fact, unless it be that the French mind is so active and so brilliant that it easily arrives at the truth. A Frenchman, if he considers the matter of government and politics, very soon arrives at his conclusion—that man has rights, and that a form of government which comes least in collision with them is the best. It is entirely a matter of theory with him. Everything tends to theory. The practical is ignored. Hence, while Paris abounds with theoretical democrats and republicans, there are few men in it capable of administering the affairs of a democratic republic.

HOTEL DES INVALIDES.

The Hotel des Invalides is visited by a vast crowd of people, Parisians, provincials, and foreigners, for it is the final resting place of Napoleon the Great. It is an imposing structure, and aside from the interest felt in it as the receptacle of the remains of Napoleon, it is well worth a visit. It is situated on the south side of the Seine, not far from the chamber of deputies, its front facing the south. It presents a magnificent appearance from the street, perhaps the finest of any like building in Europe. It has long been a celebrated military hospital for the reception of disabled and superannuated soldiers. Under Louis XIV. the present hospital was instituted, and building after building was added, together with a fine church, until the vast pile covers sixteen acres of ground, and encloses fifteen courts. At the time of the revolution, the hospital was called the Temple of Humanity, under Napoleon the Temple of Mars, and now the Hotel des Invalides. It is under the control of the minister of war, has a governor and a multiplicity of inferior officers. It is divided into fourteen sections, over each of which an officer is appointed. All soldiers who are disabled, or who have served thirty years in the army, are entitled to the privileges of the institution, and are boarded, clothed, and lodged. For breakfast they have soup, beef, and vegetables, for dinner, meat, vegetables, and cheese. They have but two meals a day. They also receive pay at the rate of two francs a day, and the officers higher in proportion to their rank. Before the northern face of the building there is a large open space, in which many trophies of war are placed, and there are beds of flowers interspersed among them. On the southern front there is a fine statue of Napoleon. The library of the hospital contains fourteen thousand volumes, and is of course open to all the inmates. The church is a very important part of the great pile of buildings, and is filled with statues of great military men, trophies of different campaigns, etc. etc. The dome of this church is one of the finest in Paris, and is decorated in the interior in a gorgeous style.

Beneath the dome lies the tomb of Napoleon, the great attraction of the place. It is, for a wonder, simple and massive in its style, and upon it are laid Napoleon's hat, sword, imperial crown, etc. etc. To this tomb thousands of admirers have come and will come to the latest generations, for whatever were the faults of the great military hero, he had the faculty of making passionate admirers. The old soldiers in the institution seem to regard the tomb as an object of adoration, and guard it as carefully as they would the living body of the hero.

Across the Seine from the Hotel des Invalides, on the avenue des Champs Elysees, is the fashionable Jardin d'Hiver, a roofed garden of hot-houses, and which is open in winter as a flower-garden. The admittance is not free, but costs a franc. It often contains very fine collections of the costliest and rarest of plants and flowers. The French exquisites in the cold and chilly weather are fond of frequenting its exhibitions, and to the stranger who would like to see the higher classes of Paris, in a public garden, it is an interesting place.

Jardin d'Hiver.

CHAPTER IX.

GUIZOT—DUMAS—SUE—THIERS—SAND.

M. GUIZOT.

PIERRE FRANCOIS GUILLAUME GUIZOT, was born at Nismes in 1787. At the age of seven years he saw his own father guillotined during the reign of terror, and without doubt this fact made a deep impression upon his heart, and led him ever after instinctively to dislike the people and a popular government. His mother took refuge in Switzerland. She was a strong Calvinist, and from her the son imbibed his rigid Calvinistic sentiments. He had no youth, properly speaking, for he was apparently devoid of youthful feeling and passions. He was educated in the strict and formal school of Geneva, and his education, together with his nature, made him a stoic, a man with no sympathies for the people, lacking heart, possessing a great intellect, and rigidly honest.

At the age of nineteeen he left Geneva for Paris, to study law, and his poverty was such that he was obliged to seek employment. M. Stopper, an old minister of the Helvetic confederation, took him as a tutor for his children. His pride rebelled against his situation, for the children of the minister were spoiled, and whenever he went into the street they made him stop before every confectioner's shop to satisfy their depraved appetites. This he refused to do, and the children made loud complaints, the result of which was, that Guizot left his place, declaring that it was not his mission to buy candies for the minister's children! In endeavoring to téach these children the grammar of their language, M. Guizot made a *Dictionary of Synonymes*, which he sold to a bookseller for a reasonable price. This was his first attempt at authorship. He made the acquaintance of M. Luard, who was the chief censor of new books, before whom his little dictionary came. M. Luard discovering in the young Guizot great talents and capacity, prevailed upon him to give up writing of synonymes, and devote himself to more honorable and lucrative labors.

Recommended by his friend, he wrote for nearly all the public journals in turn, giving them specimens of his cold, unimpassioned style, which was never after changed. He wrote *himself* upon his paper, and like himself was his style—cold and dignified. But his style had admirers, though not many readers. He was accorded genius and an exalted intellect, but he was not loved. His first books were the *Annals of Education*, *Lives of the French Poets of the Age of Louis XIV.*, and a translation of *Gibbon's Fall of the Roman Empire.* These volumes were noticed in a flattering manner by all scholars and critics, and the young author very soon occupied a high position in Paris. After this he did not seem to succeed, and he wrote a couple of pamphlets upon the condition of French literature and fine arts. He failed as a critic, and was appointed to the chair of modern history in the university. His political fortunes now commenced. His manners, his dress, which was severe in style, and his pale face, all combined to make him for the time a lion, and he drew crowds to his lectures. This was in 1812. M. Guizot was one of the first to foresee and prepare for the restoration.

M. Guizot met in society a Mademoiselle Meulan, a literary woman of note, and fancied her. She was utterly poor, and during a severe fit of illness he wrote articles which she signed, and thus earned enough for her support. When she had recovered, she gave him her heart and hand in marriage, though she had not a *sou* of dowry. She was older than he, but was a woman of many virtues. Madame Guizot was an intimate friend of the Abbe Montesquieu, who was the principal secret agent of Louis XVIII. As soon as Guizot was married, he was let into these secrets, and became private secretary to the abbe. He was in the habit of meeting the friends of the restoration every evening at a club, and he did not hesitate to take a bold part in its proceedings. Royer-Collard said to him after one of these meetings, "Guizot, you will rise high." Guizot demanded an explanation He replied, "You have ambition; you have much head but no heart; you will rise high. When the restoration comes the abbe will be minister, and he will make you secretary-general." Such was the fact eighteen months after. The Calvinistic religion of Guizot was no bar to his promotion, so long as his conscience permitted him to serve with unquestioned zeal his master, and he was never troubled on that score. The return of Napoleon from Elba was a sudden blow to the fortunes of Guizot, and he became the friend of the new minister, who kept him provisionally in office. He was suddenly dismissed, however, because, he declares, he would not sign an additional act to the constitution, but the minister denied this. He returned to Ghent, where in the *Moniteur* he published bitter articles against Napoleon and his government. The columns were filled with criticisms of this nature. He endeavored afterward to disown some of these articles, but the authorship clung to him.

Napoleon was vanquished, but Guizot continued to write books. Some of them were as follows: "*Some Ideas upon the Liberty of the Press;*" "*Of the Representative Government;*" "*Essay upon the state of Public Instruction.*" He was a *busy* man—he was never idle. This is in his favor, and undoubtedly he honestly sought the good of the nation, though mixed with this desire there was a strong love of fame, and great ambition. He wrote a book upon the elections, and the king created a new department for him—that of director-general of the communes and departments. He made use of his position to extend his influence. He became chief of the doctrinaire school, which included many eminent men of that time, and acquired great political power. It occupied a kind of middle ground between the *ancien régime* and pure liberalism. There came a reäction, and Guizot again took to his pen, leaving office and emolument. The king did not like his writings, and even his office of professor of history in the university was taken from him. He was a man who was not dejected through misfortune, and grew stronger as he was persecuted. His wife was taken very ill, and finally died. The Catholic priests endeavored to gain access to her bed-side, but were not permitted. She died a convert to Protestantism. Guizot was to her a good husband, but she always felt keenly the fact that she was older than her husband. He married a young and beautiful English woman, of whom he was passionately fond, if so cold a man ever possessed passions. His first wife, it is said, knew who was to succeed her. He now wrote a *History of Representative Government*, in which he gave the administration repeated blows.

He issued new books often enough to keep his name constantly before the public, and these volumes were loudly praised by the opposition journals. The administration modified its conduct toward him, and he again participated in public affairs. But he foresaw the great change which was coming, and this time made sure to make no blunders. Perhaps, indeed, it is probable that he was honest in desiring a government like that of Louis Phillippe—at any rate, he saw with great shrewdness the revolution, and profited by his foresight.

Guizot became the minister of Louis Phillippe. He commenced a system of corruption which long after ruined his fortunes and those of his master. It is, perhaps, difficult to say who was the soul of this system—the king or the minister; but both were heartily in it and approved it, and M. Guizot, of course, is responsible for it.

He did not forget his friends during his good fortune, but imitating Louis Phillippe, he gave place to all his old companions. His *valet de chambre*, even, was made *sous-prefet*, but this appointment raised such a storm that the king made a change in the ministry. But during his short retirement from office he never for a moment lost the ear of his royal master, who well knew the capabilities of the man—and too well to spare his services for any great length of time. The two men were suited to each other, and united their fortunes. The queen was conscious of Guizot's ambition, and it is said spoke of it to the king. But Louis Phillippe could not have expected pure devotion without hope of reward. He ruled through bribery, and could not blame a minister for being animated in his service by personal considerations. The plan of Guizot seemed to be to buy up all malcontents who could not be awed into subjection, or in fact, all who were *worth* buying. This corrupt system he carried as far as it was possible, and avoid too much scandal. He bought up constituencies for the king, and with his fellows he successfully silenced the opposition. One of his enemies was M. Thiers, who constantly persecuted him through a long course of years. The bearing of Guizot while minister, was dignified, calm, and indeed grand. He could never, by passionate attacks or bitter persecutions, be tempted into any undignified displays of temper. He was a stoic everywhere—in politics as well as in his religion, and at home. It is a singular fact that M. Guizot, who was a great minister of corruption, who bought votes by the wholesale, never allowed himself to profit pecuniarily, in the slightest degree, by his position. He did not amass a franc save by his honest earnings, and so well was his character known in this respect, that he was above al!

suspicion. He did not love money—but power. He was economical in his habits, caring nothing for idle pomp or extravagant show. While ambassador in London he walked the streets with a plain umbrella, instead of riding in his carriage, and such were his general habits of economy that he amassed a fine property.

His second wife now died, and it is said that after the event, he carried on intrigues with women; it is certain that he was very susceptible to female beauty and accomplishments. He was thought fine-looking by the ladies, and did not lack admirers among them. It is said by his enemies that he greatly admires himself, and that his home abounds with portraits of himself from chamber to kitchen. It is also told of him, to illustrate his hatred of M. Thiers, that when he was ambassador in London, he would not receive his instructions from his enemy, who was the minister in power, but received secret notes from Louis Phillippe, and in the king's own hand.

But the system adopted by the king and M. Guizot, ended in ruin. The latter saved himself by ignominious flight. He clothed himself as a peasant, and in this manner crossed the frontier. He afterward gave an eloquent description of his escape. So hurried was his departure from Paris, that he could not even bid his mother good-by. He loved her fondly; indeed his affection for her was the strongest sentiment of his heart. It was the link which connected him with humanity. His mother set out to rejoin him in London, and died on the way. It was unquestionably the hardest trial, the most dreadful shock of his life, but he was true to his stoical nature, and manifested not the sign of an emotion when the news came to him.

The king and the minister were together in England,

in exile, but they did not visit each other. They had both learned a lesson—that a system of corruption will in the end defeat itself. Since his flight to London, M. Guizot has written two or three works, but they have not had a marked success, and only prove that he clings tenaciously to his old conservative opinions.

ALEXANDER DUMAS.

Alexander Dumas, one of the most celebrated authors of France, was born on the 24th of July, 1802, in the village of Villars-Coterets. His grandfather, the marquis de la Pailletrie, was governor of the island of St. Domingo, and married a negress called Tiennette Dumas. Some declare that this woman was his mistress, and not his wife, but we will not pronounce upon this point. The marquis returned to France, bringing with him a young mulatto—the father of the subject of this sketch. The youth took the name of his mother, and entered the army as a private soldier. He soon achieved renown and rose step by step to the rank of general of a division. Under the empire, he died without fortune, leaving his son—Alexander Dumas—to the care of his widow, who was quite poor. Alexander commenced his studies under the Abbe Gregoire, who found it impossible to teach him arithmetic, and with great difficulty beat a little Latin into him. This arose, not from the boy's stupidity, but because he did not apply himself. He was exceedingly fond of outdoor sports and exercise, and to such an extent did he follow his inclinations in this particular, that he laid the foundation for a vigorous health, that years of labor have never impaired. He was very handsome when a boy, with long, curling hair, blue eyes, and a skin a little tinged with the tropical hue, to denote his African descent. At the age of eighteen, he entered a notary's office in his native village, with the purpose of studying law.

Leuven, exiled from Paris until the return of the Bourbons, resided in the village, and forming the acquintance of young Dumas and noticing that he was ambitious, he counseled him to write dramas, and he would make money. Dumas followed his advice—wrote three, which were offered to the directors of the Paris theaters, and were each rejected by all. But Dumas was made of stuff of the better sort, and was not thus to be discouraged. Leuven soon returned to Paris, and Dumas longed to follow him there. But he was too poor. He formed a plan, however, of gaining his point, for he was anxious to see and know the actors of Paris, and with a fellow-clerk he set out on foot for the great city. The two young men were without money, but each carried a gun. They shot hares and partridges as they journeyed toward Paris, and sold them to dealers in game, and thus paid their expenses from day to day.

Leuven received him with open arms, and gave the delighted youth a ticket to hear Talma. He was privileged to go behind the scenes between the acts, and converse with the actors. He was filled with delight. Talma saw him, and at once pronounced him a genius. In his memoirs, he declares that he said, "Alexander Dumas, I baptize you a poet, in the name of Shakspeare, Corneille, and Schiller. Return to your native village, enter your study, and the angel of Poesy will find you there, and will raise you by the hair, like the Prophet Habakkuk, and transport you to the spot where duty lies before you."

Alexander soon came to Paris again, not this time supporting himself by his gun, but with money which his mother gave him. He had letters of recommendation to some of the old generals of the empire, and installed himself comfortably in the *Place des Italiens.* Some of the men to whom he had letters received him coldly, but in General Foy he found a warm friend and protector. He introduced him to the notice of the duke of Orleans, who finding that the young man possessed a good hand-writing, which, by the way, he preserves to this day, he made him one of his secretaries, and gave him a salary of twelve hundred francs. Alexander now considered himself on the high road to fortune. He was in Paris—and with a salary! It was small, to be sure, but he was where he could frequent the theaters, and his patron was a man of eminence. He had little to do, and read Shakspeare, Scott, Goethe, and Schiller. He said to General Foy, "I live now by my hand-writing, but I assure you that one day I will live by my pen." This shows that he looked forward to a literary life—that he foresaw, in a measure, his after success in literature. He soon began to write, and some of his plays were so well liked by the managers of different theaters, that they bought them and brought them out. He had already, while a secretary, begun to receive money for his writings. He wrote for his mother who came up to Paris, and the couple took up their residence in a humble apartment in the faubourg St. Denis. For a time after this, his efforts were attended with poor success, but he had the good fortune to please the director-general of the theaters by a tragedy, and he promised him that it should be brought out. Before this was done the director left for the east, and in his absence the man who took his place refused to bring out the play. Dumas made loud complaint. The censor asked him if he had money, and he replied that he had not a *sou*. He demanded of him what he depended upon for his support, Dumas referred to his salary of twelve hundred francs, as secretary to the duke of Orleans. The censor advised him to stick to his writing-desk. This was not only cruel, but very unjust treatment of an author of great promise. In this play, it is but right to state, Dumas exhibited the weakness which has almost uniformly characterized his career—that of plagiarism. His situations, and sometimes his language, were stolen from Goethe, Scott, etc., etc. His next play was entitled *Henry III.*, and was brought out under the protection of the duke of Orleans. It was very successful, and he received for it the sum of fifty thousand francs. It was, like the play which preceded it, filled with stolen passages and scenes, but this did not detract from its success. He now left his humble lodgings and took up his residence in the Rue de l'University, where he lived in splendid style. He was not a man to hoard his money, but to enjoy it as it was earned.

His life at this time was almost a ludicrous one. He lived in the most luxurious manner, dressed fantastically, and loved a great number of women. After the great success of *Henry III.*, the play—*Christine*—which had previously been rejected, was brought forward with success.

In the revolution of July Dumas acted bravely, and has himself told the story of his conduct with not a little boasting. He brought out the drama of *Napoleon Bonaparte*, and that of *Charles VII.*, after Louis Philippe was upon the throne. These dramas he had the fame of writing, but other persons wrote largely in them. He adopted the plan of employing good writers upon the different parts of a drama, and while himself superintending the whole and writing prominent parts, yet entrusting to his assistants a great portion of the composition. It was his genius which arranged the plot and guided the selection of characters, but the glory should have often been divided with his humbler co-laborers. Victor Hugo wrote a play which the censors would not allow to be brought out. He read it to Dumas. The latter soon issued a play which was so very like that of Hugo, that when sometime after the interdict was taken off from the play of Hugo, he was accused of stealing from Dumas. But the truth was easily to be proved—that Hugo's play was *first* written—and Dumas declared in the public newspapers that if there was any plagiarism in anybody, himself was the guilty party! A new play now appeared which was principally written by assistants, and which was also defaced by plagiarisms. Like some of those which preceded it, it made light, indeed glorified, vices of the darkest dye.

A person by the name of Gillardet wrote a play, and presented it to the manager of a theater, who not liking it, asked Jules Janin, the critic, to revise it. Not liking it any better after the work of Janin upon it, he handed it over to Dumas for a similar revision. He reärranged it and brought it out as his own play! M. Gillardet went to law upon the matter and recovered his rights. A duel was the result of the quarrel. Many plays after this were written, until at last Janin, the critic, wrote a severe article upon one of Dumas' plays. The author was wroth, and replied. Janin made a second attack, and Paris laughed at the author. Dumas swore that he would have blood, and author and critic went on to the field for combat. Dumas demanded to fight with the sword—Janin with the pistol—and finally not coming to agreement upon this point, the parties made up their quarrel and became friends.

The reader will have seen by this time where Dumas' genius lies—it is in the arrangements for a drama—in working a subject up for the stage. It is not so much in the matter, as the manner. Give him incidents, and he will group them so as to produce a great effect. This is his power.

Dumas' income grew large, and he took a new and more princely residence. He associated himself with the great, and even went so far as to take an actress to a ball given by his patron, the duke of Orleans. The woman acted in his plays, and his relations with her were too intimate, but he soon afterward married her. They lived so extravagantly that a separation soon followed, and though Dumas' income was two hundred thousand francs a year, yet he was constantly in debt from his astonishing extravagance. He built at St. Germain his villa of Monte Christo, which required enormous sums of money. He imported two architects from Algiers, to decorate at a great expense one room after the fashion of the east, and pledged them not to execute any similar work in Europe. He has twelve reception-rooms in his house, and it is magnificently furnished throughout. He keeps birds, parrots, and monkeys, and a collection of fine horses.

From 1845 to 1846 he issued sixty volumes, the majority, of course, written *for*, not by him. As a matter of course, if these volumes sold successfully, his income was enormous, and his name upon the cover of a book seemed to insure its success. A theater was erected for the express purpose of representing his plays alone, called the Theater of History. He now visited Spain, and was present at the marriage of the duke of Montpensier. Coming home, he made a short tour in Africa, where he engaged in rare sports. He was accompanied by his son Alexander, who is a distinguished author.

After the revolution of 1848 Dumas appeared among the people, who welcomed him as a pure democrat. He started a journal which soon died. A good story is told of him about this time. A great admirer said to him that there was a gross historical error in one of his romances. "Ah!" said Dumas, "in what book?" The volume and error were pointed out, when he exclaimed, "Ah! I have not read the book. Let me see—the little Augustus wrote it. I will cut his head off!"

He got so rapidly in debt soon after this, that he left France for Brussels. Monte Christo was seized to pay his debts.

He broke off with one of the most eminent of his assistants, and since then, his romances and plays have lacked much of the interest and ability which they formerly possessed, and he is not regarded to-day as he once was in Paris. This may be owing in part to the sickly condition of literature under the despotism of Louis Napoleon. In his personal appearance he is burly; he has large, red cheeks, his hair is crisped and piled high upon his forehead. His eyes are dark, his mouth a sensuous one; his throat is generally laid bare, and in short, he is a good looking man. It is said that he has thought of visiting the United States, and would do so, were it not for the prejudice against color in America.

EUGENE SUE.

Marie-Joseph Sue, was born on the first day of January, 1801, in Paris. His family was from Provence. His great-grandfather, Pierre Sue, was a professor of medicine in the faculty of Paris, and was the author of several excellent works, but died poor. His grandfather was not a learned man, but was exceedingly wealthy. He was physician to the family of Louis XVI. His father was professor of anatomy, and was appointed by Napoleon surgeon of the Imperial Guard, and was, later, physician to the family of Louis XVIII. He was married three times, and his wives each bore him children. The second wife was the mother of the great novelist, and she died soon after giving birth to her child. The Prince Eugene and the Empress Josephine stood sponsors at the baptism of the child, and in after life he relinquished his two given names for that of Eugene—after the prince—by which he is now universally known.

While at school, Eugene and an intimate companion were noted for the mischief they wrought. One of their mischievous acts was, to raise Guinea pigs and then turn them loose in the botanical garden of the elder Sue, where, of course, they destroyed many of the plants.

A tutor was engaged to school the refractory boys—one that was very poor, and who dreaded above all things else, to lose his situation. Whenever the tutor required that the boys should study their Latin, they threatened him with a dismissal from his place, and so intimidated him by this and other means, that he was content to let them alone. The elder Sue asked him how the boys progressed in their Latin. He was compelled to reply that they were excellent scholars, whereupon the old gentleman demanded a specimen of the Latin they had acquired. They at once manufactured a torrent of atrocious sentences, and palmed them off upon him as genuine Latin, he not knowing enough to detect the imposition, but the remorseful tutor had to listen to it in silence! The father was delighted.

The elder Sue was a very easy, good-natured man, but had no learning, though he was reckoned a *savan* of the first water. Eugene knew this, and wickedly took advantage of it. His father—the doctor—was in the habit of delivering a course of botanical lectures to a circle of very select ladies, and Eugene suspected that his father, notwithing his voluble discourse, had little knowledge of botany. He, therefore, with one or two of his companions, took occasion (as it was their task to prepare plants and flowers in vases, with their names written upon the vases for examination) to insert new and unheard of names to puzzle the old man. He entered the hall one day, smiling to the ladies on either hand, and stood before them. He took up a vase, and for an instant was staggered by the name, but it would not do to let his ignorance be known, so he very coolly said, "This, ladies, is the *concrysionisoides.*" He hemmed a little, and then for more than an hour descanted upon the character and nature of the fabulous plant, it is needless to add, fabricating all the way through. Eugene was unkind enough not only to enjoy the scene, but to go and tell the ladies of the joke.

About this time, the since celebrated Dr. Veron became a fellow-pupil of Sue's, and made the fourth of this band of youthful jokers. They were now assistant surgeons in one of the Paris hospitals. Eugene one day made the discovery that in his father's cabinet there was an apartment in which he kept a very choice collection of wines, which were presents from the allied sovereigns, when they were in Paris. There were among others, sixty bottles of delicate Johannisberg, a present from Prince Metternich. The students soon found the way, led by Eugene, to this wine, and drank time after time. The question came up as to what should be done with the bottles. Eugene proposed that the empty ones be concealed, but Dr. Veron remarked that their absence would bring detection. So a plan was hit upon which was far better—the bottles were half-filled with wine and then water was added. The doctor was fond on great occasions of bringing out this old wine and telling the story connected with it, and drinking a few bottles. He thus ordered it on the table one day, and prepared his guests to expect a remarkable wine. They drank in silence, while the doctor exclaimed, "Delicious!—but *it is time it was drunk.*" Eugene was present and drank his wine and water without any emotion. But not long after, while the students were drinking the pure wine, the old doctor entered the cabinet and caught them at their wicked work. It was an act never to be forgotten by him, and he was astounded beyond measure. About this time he also discovered that Eugene had been borrowing money at usurious interest to pay debts he had contracted, and he was so indignant that he ordered him to leave his house. Eugene joined the army and went to Spain. His father became anxious for his safety, and had him attached to the staff of the duke of Augouléme. But young Sue took good care not to expose himself to much danger. He passed through the seige of Cadiz, the taking of Trocadero, and returned to Paris in safety. His father was delighted to see him, and received him kindly. But the doctor did not open his purse.

Young Sue found his old companion faring sumptuously, being attached to a liberal man named De Forges, who also supplied Sue occasionally with money. Dr. Veron drove a fine horse and tilbury, and Sue was not content until he could do the same. He applied to the Jewish money-lenders, who replied that if he would sell a lot of wines for them, they would allow him a handsome commission. As a last resort he sold the wine, and procured a fine horse and phæton. Driving out one day very rapidly in the streets, he ran down a pedestrian, and looking at the unfortunate man he discovered that it was his own father! The old man was exceedingly angry and caned him on the spot. He demanded an explanation of his son for this apparent wealth, and commanded him at once to go to Toulon and enter the military hospital there, in the practice of his profession. In Toulon his personal appearance was so fascinating that the women fell in love with him, and he carried on many shameful intrigues.

In 1825 he returned to Paris, and found an old friend of his the director of a little journal. He commenced writing articles for this little journal, some of them light and others of a *spirituel* character, which were highly admired. In Paris he was also given to intrigues with women. In 1826 he made many aristocratic conquests, and frequented the home of a celebrated female novelist. In his first romances, his high-born mistresses figure as his principal characters. The elder Sue now formally declared that he would pay no more debts of his son, and he was again reduced to poverty. He had recourse to the Jews, who lent him money upon his expectations from his grandfather. He plunged again into extravagance, and this time his father placed him as surgeon in the navy, and in this capacity he made voyages round the world. Soon after his return, his maternal grandfather died, and his father a little later left him a large fortune, and he commenced a life of gorgeous extravagance and sensuality, which has often been described. From 1831 to 1833, he published a series of sea-romances, which had a great success, and the French critics called him the French Cooper. He was very proud, frequented the most gay and fashionable circles, and assumed airs above his station. He was, however, one day excessively mortified by the sarcastic allusion of one of his noble friends to the business or profession of his father. He once more tried the pen to achieve a name for himself, and this time in history. For the Naval History of France which he wrote, he received eighty thousand francs, an enormous price for a poor book. The more renown he acquired, the less pains he took with his books, but he always made good any losses incurred by publishers in publishing his works.

Finding himself in years, he bethought himself of mar

riage, and turned his attention to a relative of of Madam de Maintenon, who refused him upon the pretext of the disparity in their ages. He had his revenge in writing against marriage, and against all aristocracies in his romances. His *Mysteries of Paris* appeared in the *Debats*, and the *Wandering Jew* in the *Constitutionel.* He endeavored through his fiction to teach Socialistic doctrines, and so far carried them into practice that he appeared in the streets in a blouse. There can be no question that his later novels were written with a far higher aim than the early ones, which were reeking with a refined, yet none the less loathsome sensuality. An enormous price was paid for the *Wandering Jew* by the editor of the *Constitutionel*, who was none other than his old companion of the wine-closet—Dr. Veron. The latter made a bargain with the author to write ten small volumes a year for fourteen consecutive years, for which he agreed to pay one hundred thousand francs a year, or nearly a million and a half for the whole engagement. He presented Dr. Veron with the manuscript of the *Seven Capital Sins*, when the worthy editor found himself drawn to the life, under the title of the Gourmand. He protested against it, but Sue pleading the bargain, would not abate one sentence. Dr. Veron would not, of course, publish it, and finally the contract was annulled. The Gourmand—Dr. Veron—was published in the *Seicle*, and the others of the *Capital Sins*, were published in the *Presse.*

Sue had at this time a splendid chateau in the environs of Orleans—the chateau des Bordes. Here he lived in great luxury and splendor. In the days of the republic he was elected a member of the legislative assembly, which office at first he was backward in assuming. In

1852 Sue sold his Orleans property, and removed to a beautiful place in Savoy, where his life was described as follows: "He rises in the morning and receives from a servant a long bamboo cane, and walks in the region of his house until breakfast. A pretty house-keeper waits upon him while he partakes of a sumptuous meal, and when it is finished, he enters his study to write. The servant presents him with a spotless pair of kid gloves in which he always writes. At each chapter a new and perfumed pair is presented him. He writes five or six hours steadily, without correcting or reading. His income is from sixty to eighty thousand francs a year from these writings. After laborious writing, Sue makes his toilet in the best style, and prepares for dinner, which is everything that an epicure might desire. After dinner he mounts a fine horse and rides among the hills which surround his home, until his digestion is completed. He returns, smokes tobacco from an amber pipe, and enjoys himself at his leisure.

Of Eugene Sue's character it is, perhaps, needless for me to make any criticisms. He has many admirers in all parts of the world—and also many enemies. That he is a romancer of astonishing powers nobody will deny, but we well may question the use he has made of those powers. Nearly all of his earlier romances are unfit for the eyes of pure men and women, and now that he is dead, let us hope that they too will perish. In later years, M. Sue has endeavored to advocate the cause of the poor, and with great eloquence, in his fictions. But he has probably caused as much harm by the licentiousness of his style, as he has accomplished good by his pleas for the poor. It is stated that he has given very liberally to the poor, and in practice exemplified his doctrine. His books give an indication of the present fashionable morality of Paris and France, and though they have sold largely in America, their influence cannot be good.

M. THIERS.

M. Thiers has figured prominently in French politics, was a minister of Louis Phillippe, and is a historian. He is a man of a singular nature, witty and eccentric, rather than profound and dignified, and it will not do to pas him by without a notice. He was born in Marseilles, in the year 1797. His father was a common workman, but his mother was of a commercial family which had been plunged into poverty by a reverse of fortune. The young Thiers was educated through the bounty of the state, at the school of Marseilles, and was, when a boy, known principally for his rogueries. He sold his books to get apples and barley-sugar. Punishments seemed never to have any terror for him. At one time he concealed a tom-cat in his desk in the school, with its claws confined in walnut shells, and suddenly in school hours let him loose, to the great astonishment and anger of his teachers. He was condemned to a dungeon for eight days, and received a terrible reprimand. The effect of either the lecture or the imprisonment was decided. He became docile and obedient, and paid attention to his studies. For seven years he studied with unremitting attention, and during all that time took the first prizes of his class. He now went to Aix to study law, where his old habits returned to him, and he became wild and mischievous in his ways. At eighteen Adolphe Thiers was a favorite with the liberals and a terror to the royalists, and was the leader of a party at Aix. He already showed fine powers of oratory and composition, which later conducted him to power. He spoke and wrote in the interest of the enemies of the restoration. He wrote for the newspapers whose columns were open to him, and increased the vigor and eloquence of his style by this constant practice.

There was at Aix an academy which awarded prizes to the best writers upon given subjects. Thiers wrote for the prize, but was foolish enough to reserve a copy of his treatise and read it to his companions, who loudly proclaimed that he must win. The persons who were to award the prizes were royalists, and hated Thiers for his liberalism, and when they heard the vauntings of Thiers' friends, they were prepared to decide against him, which they did when the day of examination came. The prize was reserved, and another trial was instituted. Thiers put in his old treatise, and this time the judges awarded to it the second prize, and gave *the first* for a treatise which came to them from Paris. Judge of their chagrin when they found that this treatise was written by Thiers! The little student had fairly taken them in his net. Great were the rejoicings of the liberals in Aix.

Among the friends of Thiers was Mignet, since a historian, and the young men full of hope came together to Paris, where, poor as they were hopeful, they took lodgings in a miserable street. Mignet determined to follow literature and by it gain a living and fame, but Thiers resolved upon intrigue. He made himself known to the liberal leaders, and with great tact exhibited his abilities. He was instantly offered employment of various kinds, and chose that of editor. He took charge of the *Constitutionel*, and plunged into the heat and strife of party politics. His witty, hornet-like nature fitted him well for the position. He attained great influence and power, and the great men of the time, even Talleyrand, came to him, while he exclaimed bombastically and blasphemously, "Suffer little children to come unto me."

He went into society, made the acquaintance of the old men of the revolution, and gathered the materials for the *History of the Revolution*, which afterward carried him to the height of his popularity. He fought two duels about this time—one with the father of a young lady whom he had seduced. He started a new journal called the *National*, which should be more fully under his control than the *Constitutionel* had been, and which should entirely meet his views of what a journal should be. But the new journal seriously offended the government, the officers of which attempted to put it down, for on the morning of the 26th of July, they nearly destroyed the presses of the establishment. The opposition journalists had a meeting to express their opinions upon this outrage upon the rights of the press. During the three troublous days of fighting, Thiers left Paris for the suburbs, and came back in time to make his fortune, for he was soon named secretary-general to the government. He had the principal management of the finances, which at that time were in a state of great disorder. Thiers delivered a public speech upon the law of mortgages, and Royer-Collard approached him with open arms, exclaiming, "Your fortune is made!"

In the meantime, M. Thiers, as the holidays were approaching, thought it wise to run down to Aix, which he represented in the chamber of deputies. Since he was last there he had changed his course upon many of the important questions of the day. Formerly he was extremely liberal, but for the sake of power he had deserted the cause of Poland and Italy.

He let the inhabitants of Aix know that he was coming, that no excuse might be wanting for a grand reception. Surely the people of Aix would feel proud of their fellow-citizen who had been so highly honored by the government!

He arrived before the gates of the town and was surprised at the silence everywhere. No crowd came out to greet him—the people were about their business. A few officials alone met and welcomed him back to the scene of his early triumphs. He went to his hotel, and when night came, it was told him that crowds of people were gathered in the street below. He went to the window—ah! now the people were come to do him honor! What was his chagrin to hear the multitudes commence a serenade of the vilest description. Tin horns were blown, tin pans were pounded, and every species of execrable noise was made, and M. Thiers came to the conclusion that the people of Aix did not admire his late political conduct. To satisfy him, the leaders cried aloud, "Traitor to Poland.

to Italy, and France!" He was satisfied, and hurried back to Paris, where Louis Phillippe met him, and as if to console him for his reception in Aix, gave him a portfolio—and he was the king's minister.

One of his first acts was to destroy the character of the duchess of Berri, who pretended that the French throne belonged to her son. Louis Phillippe gave him almost unlimited power to accomplish this object, and he set to work coolly and with deliberate calculation. It is said he bribed an intimate friend of the duchess, who knew where she was, with a million of francs to betray her, and she was thrown into prison. Once there, he found means to ruin her fame and destroy her influence, though the measures he took excited the indignation of France. He extorted from her a secret confession, under the promise that it should always remain strictly secret, and then coolly published it in the government organ.

Under M. Thiers the finances of the country improved, and many of the public works were completed. The splendid Quai d'Orsay and the Place Vendome were finished, and the Madeleine begun. At the ceremonies which attended the inauguration of the column upon the Place Vendome, a good thing was said in the ears of the minister by a Parisian wit. Thiers was at the foot of the column—the statue of Napoleon at the top. The height of the column is one hundred and thirty-two feet. Said the wit aloud, "There are just one hundred and thirty-two feet from the ridiculous to the sublime!"

But M. Thiers was not in reality a ridiculous man. Under his management France saw prosperity. He developed its resources and exhibited great abilities. He was constantly subjected to attacks from his old radical associates and he deserved them. The great quarrel of his life, however, was with Guizot. These two men were constantly by the ears with each other, and the king gave one a certain office and the other another. He changed these officers from time to time, until at last both saw that one alone must triumph. Guizot was the triumphant man, and Thiers fell. He became more radical as he lost office, and published (in 1845) two volumes of his *History of the Consulate*. They had a splendid success; he sold the whole work for five hundred thousand francs—an enormous price. But the concluding volumes were not forthcoming, and the publisher demanded them—but in vain. For the last thirty years M. Thiers has lived in a beautiful house in the place Saint Georges. He is wealthy, and has always lived in good style.

It is currently reported that M. Thiers has been guilty of treating certain members of his family with great meanness, and in society many scandalous stories have been repeated illustrating his miserly economy.

When the revolution of 1848 broke out, M. Thiers ran away from Paris, but afterward returned, and has since lived a very quiet life.

GEORGE SAND.

One of the most distinguished of the living writers of France is Madam Dudevant, or GEORGE SAND, which is her *nom de plume.* She is by no means a woman either after my ideal or the American ideal, but is a woman of great genius. Her masculinity, and, indeed, her licentious style, are great faults; but in sketching some of the most brilliant of French writers, it would not do to omit her name.

The maiden name of George Sand was Amantine Aurore Dupin, and she is descended from Augustus the Second, king of Poland. Her ancestors were of king's blood, and the more immediate of them were distinguished for their valor and high birth. She was born in the year

1804. She was brought up by her grandmother, at the chateau Nahant, situated in one of the most beautiful valleys of France. The old countess of Horn, her grandmother, was a woman of brilliant qualities, but not a very safe guide for a young child. Her ideas were anti-religious, and she was a follower of Rousseau rather than of Christ. When Aurore was fifteen years old, she knew well how to handle a gun, to dance, to ride on horseback, and to use a sword. She was a young Amazon, charming, witty, and yet coarse. She was fond of field sports, yet knew not how to make the sign of the cross. When she was twenty years old she was sent to a convent in Paris, to receive a religious education. She loved her grandmother to adoration, and the separation cost her a great deal of suffering. She often alludes in her volumes to this grandparent, in terms of warm love and veneration. In her "*Letters of a Traveller*" she gives us some details of her life with her grandmother at the chateau de Nahant. She says:

"Oh, who of us does not recall with delight the first books he devoured! The cover of a ponderous old volume that you found upon the shelf of a forgotten closet —does it not bring back to you gracious pictures of your young years? Have you not thought to see the wide meadow rise before you, bathed in the rosy light of the evening when you saw it for the first time? Oh! that the night should fall so quickly upon those divine pages, that the cruel twilight should make the words float upon the dim page!

"It is all over; the lambs bleat, the sheep are shut up in their fold, the cricket chirps in the cottage and field. It is time to go home.

"The path is stony, the bridge narrow and slippery, and the way is difficult.

"You are covered with sweat, but you have a long walk, you will arrive too late, supper will have commenced.

"It is in vain that the old domestic whom you love will retard the ringing of the bell as long as possible; you will have the humiliation of entering the last one, and the grandmother, inexorable upon etiquette, will reprove you in a voice sweet but sad—a reproach very light, very tender, which you will feel more deeply than a severe chastisement. But when, at night, she demands that you account for your absence, and you acknowledge, blushing, that in reading in the meadow you forgot yourself, and when you are asked to give the book, you draw with a trembling hand from your pocket—what? *Estelle et Nemorin.*

"Oh then the grandmother smiles!

"You regain your courage, your book will be restored to you, but another time you must not forget the hour of supper.

"Oh happy days! O my valley Noire! O Corinne! O Bernardin de Saint Pierre! O the Iliad! O Milleroye! O Atala! O the willows by the river! O my departed youth! O my old dog who could not forget the hour of supper, and who replied to the distant ringing of the bell by a dismal howl of regret and hunger!"

In other portions of her books George Sand refers to her early life, and always in this enthusiastic manner.

Her grandmother exercised no surveillance upon her reading—she perused the pages of Corinne, Atala, and Lavater, and the two former would raise strange dreams in the head of a girl only fourteen years old. She read everything which fell in her way.

In reading Lavater's essays upon Physiogomy, she noticed the array of ridiculous, hideous, and grotesque pictures, and wished to know what they were for. She saw underneath them the words—drunkard—idler—glutton, etc. etc. She very soon remarked that the drunkard resembled the coachman, the cross and meddling person the cook, the pedant her own teacher, and thus she proved the infallibility of Lavater!

Once, when in the convent at Paris, she was misled by the poetry of Catholicism, and abandoned herself to the highest transports of religious fervor. She passed whole hours in ecstasy at the foot of the altar. This shows the susceptibility of her imagination. About this time her grandmother died, and she left the convent to close the eyes of her much-loved grandparent. She returned, with the full determination of becoming religious. All the authority of her family was required to break this resolution, and, six months after, to prevail upon her to marry M. le baron Dudevant, the man they had sought out to be her husband. He was a retired soldier and a gentleman farmer. The union was a very unhappy one. She was sensitive, proud, and passionate, while he was cold, and entirely swallowed up in his agricultural pursuits. The dowry of Aurore amounted to one hundred thousand dollars, and this money M. Dudevant spent with a lavish hand upon his farm, but bestowed little attention upon his wife. At first she endured this life, for two children were given to her to alleviate her sorrows. But finding her lot grow more sad, and her health failing, she was ordered to taste the waters of the Pyrenees, whither she went, but without her husband. She rested at Bordeaux, and there made her entrance into society, through some kind friends residing in that city. She was received with praises. A wealthy shipping merchant fell deeply in love with her; she did not give way to it, however, but returned to her family, where she found no affection to welcome her.

Jules Sandeau, a student of law, spent one of his vacations at the chateau Nahant, and was the first person who turned Madame Dudevant's attention to literary pursuits. He returned to Paris profoundly in love with the lady, though he had not dared to mention it. M. Nerard, a botanist, came also to the chateau, to give lessons to M. Dudevant, and his wife was charmed with him, and they spent happy hours together. But in time love grew out of the intimacy—a love which of course was wicked, but which according to French ideas, was innocent. The husband was justly suspicious, and a voluntary separation took place, he retaining all her property in exchange for her liberty, which he gave her, and she set out for Bordeaux. She recounts a part of her subsequent history in "*Indiana*." She found her lover in Bordeaux, but he had changed, and was on the eve of marriage, and she went to Paris. She returned to the same convent where she had spent a part of her youth, to weep over her lot. She soon left the convent for an attic in the Quai St. Michel, where Jules Sandeau, the law-student, soon discovered her. She was in very destitute circumstances, and Sandeau was also very poor. She knew a little of painting, and obtained orders of a toyman to paint the upper part of stands for candlesticks, and the covers of snuff-boxes. This was fatiguing but not remunerative, and they wrote to the editor of the *Figaro* newspaper. He replied, and invited them to visit him at his home, where he received them with kindness. When Aurore spoke of her snuff-boxes, he laughed heartily; "but," said he to Sandeau, "why do not you become a journalist? It is less difficult thar you think."

Sandeau replied, "I am too slow for a journalist."

"Good!" replied Aurore; "but I will help you!"

"Very good!" replied the editor; "but work, and bring me your articles as soon as you can."

Madame Dudevant laid aside her pencil and took up the pen—not to lay it down again. She commenced a series of articles which puzzled the Parisian press. The editor liked them, but desired that she should try her hand at romance. In about six weeks Madame Dudevant and Jules Sandeau had completed a volume entitled "*Rose and Blanche, or the Comedian and the Nun;*" but they could find no publisher. The editor came to their aid, and persuaded an old bookseller to give them four hundred francs for the manuscript. When the book was to be published, they deliberated upon the name of the author. *She* disliked the scandal of authorship—*he* feared his father's curse; and the editor advised that the name of the law-student should be divided, and no friend would recognize the name. So the story came out as written by Jules Sand.

The young people thought their fortunes made—that the four hundred francs were inexhaustible. Madame Dudevant now adopted a man's costume for the first time, that she might go to the theater with advantage—at least this was her excuse. The young couple visited the theater at night, and Sandeau slept the days away. The money soon was gone, and Madame Dudevant in her new extremity was advised to return to the chateau Nahant, and endeavor to get a legal separation from her husband, and an annual allowance. When she set out, she left with Sandeau the plan of "*Indiana.*" They were to divide the chapters of the new story; but when she came back he had not written a line of his task. To his great surprise Aurore put into his hands the whole of the manuscript of the book.

"Read," said she, "and correct!" He read the first chapter, and was full of praise. "It needs no revision," he said; "it is a master-piece!" He then declared that as he had not written any of the book, he would not allow the common name to be used. She was greatly troubled, and had recourse to the editor. He proposed that she still keep the name of Sand, but select another first name. "Look in the calendar," said he; "to-morrow is the day of St. George; take the name of George—call yourself George Sand!" And this is the origin of that distinguished name.

"*Indiana*" was purchased for six hundred francs, but it sold so well that the publisher afterwards gave her a thousand francs more. The editor of *Figaro* put two of his critics upon the book to review it. They both condemned it as mediocre and without much interest. But the book had a wonderful success, and Paris was thrown into a state of excitement about the author. The journals added fuel to the fire by their remarks and criticisms, and at once Madame Dudevant was a great authoress. She took elegant apartments, where she received the artists and authors of the gay city, herself arrayed in a man's costume, and she astonished her male friends by smoking and joking with them like a man. She was known only by the name of George Sand, and preferred to be called simply George. She walked the Boulevards in a close fitting riding coat, over the collar of which fell her dark, luxuriant curls. She carried in one hand her riding whip and in the other her cigar, which from time to time she would raise to her mouth. Jules Sandeau was forgotten, and fled to Italy. In after years George Sand bitterly repented her neglect of this friend, and she has written very touchingly in one of her books her repentance. She now wrote two or three other stories which were caught up eagerly by the publishers. She wrote against the institution of marriage and the critics at once attacked her, and with justice. Story followed story from 1835 to 1837—each filled with passionate, magnificent writing, and selling with great rapidity. Her style was brilliant and elegant, and appealed to the French taste with great success.

In 1836 George Sand assumed her old name, that she might demand from her husband her fortune and children. It was proved upon trial that he had treated her with brutality in the presence of her children, and in her absence had lived shamefully, and the judge gave back to Madame Dudevant her children and her fortune. The children accompanied their mother to Paris, where she superintended their education. She now became intimate with M. Lamnenais and went so far as to repudiate the bad sentiments of many of her books. An end however soon came to her friendship for Lamnenais, and they separated in anger, and hating each other heartily. She now wrote and published several Socialistic novels, which met with a poor sale in comparison with that of some of her previous works. In fact, for the last ten years, her works have been decreasing in sale. In the revolution of 1848, George Sand took side with the republicans. At present she resides almost entirely at the chateau Nahant, where she has erected a little theater in which her pieces (for she wrote for the stage) are acted previous to their being brought out in Paris. Her income is from ten to twelve thousand francs a year, and her life is pleasant and patriarchal. She gathers the villagers round her, invites them to her table, and instructs them. She once took into her house a woman covered with leprosy, who was cast off by all others, and with her own hand ministered to her wants, dressed her sores, and nursed her until she was cured. George Sand lives in a plain style, clinging to everything which recalls her early life and her love of early friends. She sleeps but five or six hours. At eleven the breakfast bell rings. Her son Maurice presides at the table in her absence. She eats little, taking coffee morning and evening. The most of her time she devotes to literary labors. After breakfast she walks in the park; a little wood bordering upon a meadow is her favorite promenade. After half an hour's walk she returns to her room, leaving every one to act as he pleases. Dinner takes place at six, which is a scene of more careful etiquette than the breakfast table. She walks again after dinner, and returns to the piano, for she is fond of music. The evening is spent in pleasant intercourse with her guests. Sunday is given up to a public theatrical representation for the people. Such is a specimen of the life of this woman.

CHAPTER X.

PERE LA CHAISE—PRISONS—FOUNDLINGS—CHARITABLE INSTITUTIONS—LA MORGUE—NAPOLEON AND EUGENIA—THE BAPTISM.

PERE LA CHAISE.

Pere la Chaise is not a cemetery which suits my taste, but it is unquestionably the grandest in all France, and I ought not to pass it by without a few remarks upon it. I visited it but once, and then came away displeased with its magnificence. It seems to me that a cemetery should not be so much a repository of art, as a place of great natural beauty and quiet, where one would long to rest after "life's fitful fever."

The cemetery is beyond the eastern limits of the city, upon the side of a hill which commands a very fine view of the country, and is surrounded by beautiful hills and valleys. It was much celebrated in the fourteenth century, and during the reign of Louis XIV. Pere la Chaise resided upon the spot, and for a century and a half it was the country-seat of the Jesuits. Hence its name. It was purchased by the prefect of the Seine for one hundred and sixty thousand francs, for a cemetery, it then containing forty-two acres of ground. It was put into competent hands, and was very much improved by the planting of trees, laying out of roads, etc. etc. In 1804 it was consecrated, and in May of that year the first grave was made in it. It is now filled with the graves of some of the most distinguished men of Paris and France, and is by far the most fashionable cemetery in France. It is distinguished for the size, costliness, and grandeur of its monuments. There are temples, sepulchral chapels, mausoleums, pyramids, altars, and urns. Within the railings which surround many of the graves, are the choicest of flowers, which are kept flourishing in dry seasons by artificial supplies of water. A canal conducts water from a distance to the cemetery.

The day was fine, the sky cloudless when I visited the spot, and though I could not but contrast it with Mount Auburn near Boston, or Greenwood near New York, yet I was much impressed with the natural beauty of the situation. Art is, however, too profusely displayed upon the spot, and the original beauty is covered up to a certain extent. The gateway struck me as being rather pretentious. Passing through it and by the guardian's lodge, which is at its side, one of the first spots I sought was the grave of Abelard and Heloise. The stranger always asks first for it, and visits it last when returning from the cemetery. It is the most beautiful monument in the cemetery. It consists of a chapel formed out of the ruins of the Abbey of Paraclete, which was founded by Abelard, and of which Heloise was the first abbess. It is fourteen feet in length, by eleven in breadth, and is twenty-four feet in height. A pinnacle rises out of the roof in a cruciform shape, and four smaller ones exquisitely sculptured stand between the gables. Fourteen columns, six feet high, support beautiful arches, and the cornices are wrought in flowers. The gables of the four fronts have trifoliate windows, and are exquisitely decorated with figures, roses, and medalions of Abelard and Heloise. In the chapel is the tomb built for Abelard by Peter the Venerable, at the priory of St. Marcel. He is represented as in a reclining posture, the head a little inclined and the hands joined. Heloise is by his side. On one side of the tomb, at the foot, are inscriptions, and in other unoccupied places. I lingered long at this tomb, and thought of the singular lives of that couple whose history will descend to the latest generations. It seemed strange that two lovers who lived in the middle of the twelfth century, should, simply by the astonishing force of their passions, have made themselves famous " for all time." It seemed wonderful that the story of their love and shame should have so burned itself into the forehead of Time, that he carries it still in plain letters upon his brow, that the world may read. It shows how much the heart still controls the world. Love is the master-passion, and so omnipotent is it, that yet in all hearts the story of a man or woman who simply *loved each other* hundreds of years ago, calls forth our tears to-day, as if it occurred but yesterday. Bad as Abelard's character must seem to be to the careful reader—cruel as was his treatment of Heloise —he must have had depths of love and goodness of which the world knew not. Such a woman as Heloise could not have so adored any common man, nor a wonderful man who had a hard heart. She saw and knew the recesses of his heart, and pardoned his occasional acts of cruelty. Having known what there was of good and nobleness in his nature, she was willing to die, nay, to live in torture for his sake.

The tomb is constantly visited, and flowers and immortalities are heaped always over it. Had it no history to render the spot sacred, the beauty of the monument alone would attract visitors, and I should have been repaid for my visit. The French, who magnify the passion of love, or pretend to do so, at all times above all others keep the history of Abelard and Heloise fresh in their hearts.

One of the best monuments in Pere la Chaise, is that erected in memory of Casimir Périer, prime minister in 1832. It consists of an excellent statue of the statesman, placed upon a high and noble pedestal. There is a path which winds round the foot of the slope, which is by far the most beautiful in the cemetery. It is full of exquisite views, and is lined with fine monuments. Ascending the hill west of the avenue, I soon was among the tombs of the great. One of the first which struck my eye was the column erected to the memory of viscount de Martignac, who is celebrated for the defense of his old enemy, the Prince Polignac, at the bar of the chamber of peers, after the 1830 revolution. Next to it, or but a short distance from it, I saw the tomb of Volney, the duke Decrés, and the abbe Sicard, the celebrated director of the deaf and dumb school of Paris, and whose fame is wide as the world. Many others follow, each commemorating some great personage, but the majority of the names were unfamiliar to me. Among those which were known, were those of the Russian countess Demidoff. It is a beautiful temple of white marble, the entablature supported by ten columns, under which is a sarcophagus with the arms of the princes engraved upon it. Manuel, a distinguished orator in the chamber of deputies, and General Foy, have splendid monuments. Benjamin Constant has a plain, small tomb, as well as Marshal Ney.

West of these tombs lie the remains of marchioness de Beauharnais, sister-in-law of the Empress Josephine. Moliere has also near to it a fine monument; La Fontaine a cenotaph with two bas-reliefs in bronze, illustrating two of his fables. Madame de Genlis has a tomb in this quarter Her remains were transported here by Louis Phillippe. Laplace, the great astronomer, has a beautiful tomb of white marble. An obelisk is surmounted by an urn, which is ornamented with a star encircled by palm-branches. The marquis de Clermont has a fine monument—he who gallantly threw himself between Louis XVI. and the mob, to save his sovereign.

In one part of the cemetery I noticed many English tombs, of persons, I suppose, who were residents of Paris, or who visiting it were stricken by death.

One of the most superb monuments in the cemetery is that of M. Aguado, a great financier, but it smacks too strongly of money to suit my taste. He was a man of enormous wealth, therefore he has a magnificent monument. According to this method, the rich men of the world shall have monuments which pierce the skies, while the men of genius and of great and noble character, shall go without a slab to indicate their final resting-place.

This plan of turning a cemetery into a field for the display of splendid marbles, is certainly not consonant with good taste. It is calculated that in forty years not less than one hundred millions of francs have been spent in the erection of monuments in Pere la Chaise, the number of tombs already amounting to over fifteen thousand.

In 1814, when the allied forces were approaching Paris, heavy batteries were planted in Pere la Chaise, commanding the plain which extends to Vincennes. The walls had loop-holes, and the scholars of Alfort occupied it and defended it against three Russian attacks. The last was successful, and the Russians were masters of the field. The city of Paris capitulated that very evening, and the Russian troops encamped among the tombs.

PARIS FROM MONTMARTRE.

COLUMN OF JULY 8—PLACE JUILLET.

In coming back from Pere la Chaise, I saw the Column of July, erected in memory of the victims of the July of the great revolution. Upon this spot the old Bastille stood, and the column indicates it

---

THE PRISONS.

The public prisons of Paris are nine in number: for persons upon whom a verdict has not been pronounced, and against whom an indictment lies; for debt; for political offenses; for persons sentenced to death or the hulks; for criminals of a young age; for females; and for offenders in the army.

In the penal prisons, the inmates are allowed books and the privilege of writing, but are all obliged to labor, each, if he wishes, choosing the trade in which he is fitted best to succeed. The men receive a pound and a half of bread per day, and the women a fraction less.

The prison La Force is in the Rue du Roi de Sicile. The buildings of which it is composed were once the hotel of the duke de La Force—hence the name. It was converted into a prison in 1780. A new prison for prostitutes was erected about the same time, and was called La Petite Force. In 1830 the two prisons were united, and put under one management, and the whole prison is given up to males committed for trial. The prisoners are divided into separate classes; the old offenders into one ward, the young and comparatively innocent into another; the old men into one apartment, and the boys into another. The prisoners sleep in large and well ventilated chambers, and the boys have each a small apartment which contains a single bed. The prisoners have the privilege of working if they wish, but they are not obliged to do so, inasmuch as they are not yet *convicted* of crime. There is a department for the sick, a bathing-room, a parlor, and an advocate's room, where the prisoners can hold conversations with their legal defenders. The number of prisoners is very great—ten thousand being under the annual average confined in the prisons.

St. Lazare is a prison for women under indictment and those who have been sentenced to a term less than one year. One department of the prison, which is entirely separated from the rest, is devoted to prostitutes, and another distinct department is devoted to girls under sixteen years of age. Each department has its own infirmary, and a new plan has been adopted to stimulate the inmates to industry. They are allowed two-thirds pay for all the work they will perform in the prison. Every kind of manufacture is carried on in the prison—the preparation of cashmere yarn, hooks and eyes, etc. etc. The number confined in this prison in a year, is over ten thousand. The service of the prison is carried on by the sisters of charity.

La Nouvelle Force is a new prison in a healthier quarter than La Force, and is used for the same purposes. It contains twelve hundred and sixty separate cells.

Depôt de Condemnés is in the Rue de la Roquette, and is a prison for the confinement of persons condemned to forced labor and to death. It is a very healthy prison and one of the strongest in the world. A double court surrounds the prison, in which sentinels are constantly kept on guard; the walls are very thick and solid, and each prisoner has a separate cell. A fountain in the center dispenses water to all parts of the prison. The number of the inmates is at least four hundred on the average.

The Prison of Correction, situated also in Rue de la Roquette, is for the confinement and correction of offenders under the age of sixteen, who have been pronounced by the judge incapable of judgment. They are subjected to a strict, but not cruel discipline, in this prison. It is very healthy, and all its appointments are such as to facilitate the education of the morals and intellect of the inmates. It is well supplied with water and wholesome diet, and books and religious teachers. It is divided into separate departments, and one grade of boys is never allowed intercourse with another. This is a very wise regulation, as under it a fresh, ignorant, and wicked inmate cannot have influence over those who have long been under the discipline of the place.

The Conciergerie is used to confine persons before trial, and it is one of the most famous (or infamous) prisons in the world. Its historical associations are full of interest. Its entrance is on the Quai de l'Horloge. In visiting this prison, the stranger from the new world is struck with the terrible outlines of some of the apartments. The Salle des Gardes of St. Louis, has a roof which strikes terror into the heart, it is so old and grim. In one part of the building there is a low prison-room, where those persons condemned to death spend their last hours, fastened down to a straight waistcot. The little room in which Marie Antoinette was confined, is still shown to the visitor. There are now three paintings in it which represent scenes in the last days of her life. The prison-room which confined Lourel, who stabbed the duke de Barry, and the dungeons in which Elizabeth, the sister of Louis XVI., was imprisoned, are shut up and cannot be seen. There are many histories connected with this old prison, which to repeat, would fill this volume.

The Prison de l'Abbaye is a military prison, and is situated close to St. Germain des Pres. It was formerly one of the most famous in Paris, and the horrors which it witnessed during the bloody revolution were never surpassed in any city of the world. Many of the atrocities which were committed in it are now widely known through the histories of those times of blood. Many of its dungeons are still under ground, and wear an aspect of gloom sufficient to terrify a man who spends but a few moments in them. The discipline of this prison is very rigid, as it contains only military offenders.

The prison for debtors is in Rue de Clichy, and is in an airy situation, is well constructed, and holds three or four hundred persons. The officers of this prison still remember the modest-faced American editor, who spent a few memorable days in it—I mean Horace Greeley of the *Tribune.* France is not sufficiently enlightened yet to abolish imprisonment for debt, but the time will soon come. Such a barbarity cannot for any great length of time disgrace the history of any civilized nation.

The prison of St. Pelagie, in Rue de la Chef, was formerly a prison for debtors, but is now used for the imprisonment of persons committed for trial, or those persons sentenced for short terms. Nearly six hundred persons are confined in it.

Connected with the prisons of Paris are two benevolent institutions, the object of which is to watch over and educate the young prisoners of both sexes during their terms of imprisonment, and after they have left prison. As soon as they have left prison they are cared for, and if they conduct themselves well, they are generally furnished with good places. Prisoners are also taken from the Correctional House before their terms have expired, in cases of excellent conduct, and the government pays the society a sum toward the expenses of such persons until the time of their sentence shall have expired. Lamartine, the poet, was at one time president of one of these truly benevolent societies.

The prisons of Paris, take them as a whole, compare favorably with those of any city in the world. Their administration is characterized by an enlightened liberality and philanthropy, and though it may seem strange, yet it is true, that Paris abounds with the most self-sacrificing philanthropists. The prisoner, the deaf and dumb, the blind and the idiotic, are cared for with a generosity and skill not surpassed in any other land.

FOUNDLING HOSPITALS.

There are at least one hundred and fifty foundling hospitals in France, and Paris has a celebrated one in the Rue d'Enfer. It was established by St. Vincent de Paule, in 1638, but has been very much improved since. The buildings are not remarkable for their architectural beauty, for they are very plain. The chapel contains a statue of the founder. It is now necessary for a mother who desires to abandon her child, to make a certificate to that effect before the magistrate. The latter is obliged to grant the desire of the woman, though it is a part of his duty to remonstrate with her upon her unnatural conduct, and if she consents to keep the child, he is empowered to help her to support it from a public fund. The infants received at the hospital are, if healthy, put out at once to nurse in the country, and the parentage of the child is recorded. Unhealthy children are kept under hospital treatment. Nurses from the country constantly present themselves for employment, and do not usually receive more than one or two dollars a month for their trouble. After two years of nursing, the child is returned and transferred to the department for orphans. There are a little short of three hundred children in the hospital, and as many as thirteen thousand constantly out at nurse in the country. The internal arrangements of the hospital are very ingenious and good. Every convenience which can add to the comfort of the infants is at hand, and the deserted little beings are rendered much more comfortable than one would naturally suppose to be within the range of possibility.

The hospital for orphans is in the same building, and is well arranged. The orphan department and the foundling hospital, are under the special care of the sisters of charity.

There is, perhaps, no more strange sight in all Paris, than the assemblage of babies in the apartments of the Foundling Hospital. To see them ranged around the walls of the rooms in cradles, attended by the nurses, will excite a smile, and yet, when we reflect how sad is the lot of these innocents, the smile will vanish. They are deprived of that to which, by virtue of existence, every human being is entitled—a home, and the affectionate care of father and mother. To be entirely shut out from all these blessings, really makes existence a curse, and it were better if these thousands had never been born.

On visiting the hospital, I rang a bell and was admitted by a polite porter, and a female attendant conducted us through the various apartments. I was at once struck with the exceeding tidiness of everything. The floors were of polished oak, and the walls of plaster polished like glass. One of the first rooms we were shown into contained forty or fifty babies, ranged in rows along the wall. The cradles were covered with white drapery, and their appearance was very neat. Four long rows stretched across the apartment, and in the center there was a fire, round which the nurses were gathered, attending to the wants of the hungry and complaining babies. But if the sight of the cradles was pleasant, the noise which greeted my ear was far otherwise. At least twenty-five of the children were crying all at once, and *one* is as much as I can usually endure, and not that for any length of time. Among the children round the fire, there was one which was very beautiful. It had black hair and eyes, and when we stopped before it, it laughed and crowed at a great rate. I could not help wondering that any human mother could have abandoned so beautiful a babe—one that would have been "a well-spring of pleasure" in many a home.

I was next shown into the apartment for children afflicted with diseases of the eye. The room was carefully shaded, and the cradles were covered with blue or green cloth. There was quite a number of children in this department, and all of them seemed to be well cared for. I was shown into another apartment devoted entirely to the sick children, and its appointments were excellent. It was wholesome and clean, the air was pure as that of the country, and the rooms were high and commodious. Other apartments are shown to the visitor which contain the linen used in the hospital, and where all kinds of work are performed, and finally, the pretty little chapel which I have alluded to before.

In former times the government made it easy for any mother to resign her infant to the care of the state. This was done properly and with a good object in view, which was to prevent infanticide. It was intended that mothers should not only find it easy to cast off their children in this manner, but that it might be done with secrecy. A box was placed outside of the hospital and a bell-handle was near it, and all that the mother had to do was, to place her babe in the box and pull the bell. No one saw her, no questions could be asked, and the box sliding upon grooves was drawn inside the wall. The mother could leave some mark upon the dress of the child, or if this was not done, an exact inventory of the effects of the little stranger was always recorded in the hospital, that in after years the child might be identified by its parents if they wished. The numbers that were deposited in the Paris hospital were very great under those pleasant regulations. It is not strange, and one cannot escape the conviction, that such a system afforded a temptation to the women, and indeed men of the good classes to sin. A woman might escape to a great extent the penalty of a wicked deed. It held out a premium to immorality. But on the other hand it prevented infanticide to a great extent. The reasons why the government revoked the regulations were, first, that they encouraged the increase of illegitimate children, and second, the great expense to the state, and the last consideration was the one which had most weight.

It was found upon trying the new system, that infanticide increased with considerable rapidity, as the morning exhibitions at La Morgue greatly indicated. When we consider, too, that the majority of the infanticides are unquestionably not detected, the body of the child being hid from the sight, and the vast amount of injury which results to the mothers from the attempt to destroy un born children, we cannot wonder that French philanthropists have been inclined to return to the old system. Infanticide is one of the most horrible of crimes, and its growth among a people is accompanied by as rapid a growth of vice of every other kind. In England where a foundling hospital could not be endured for a moment, the crime of infanticide is increasing every year, and the number of murdered children is already an army of martyrs.

The safest way is, perhaps, for the government to leave the whole matter with the people, and not either encourage illegitimacy or attempt to prevent infanticide, except by punishment. Upon the heads of the guilty ones be their own blood. But there certainly should be asylums for those children who cannot be supported by their poverty-stricken parents.

CHARITABLE INSTITUTIONS.

Paris abounds with charitable societies and institutions. Until the latter part of the last century, the city was full of objects of compassion, the blind, the deaf and dumb, the sick and suffering. The prisons too, and the madhouses, were scenes of cruelty and violence. But a controversy arose upon the whole matter, and under Louis XVI. four new hospitals were ordered to be erected, but in the excitement which preceded the great revolution, they were not completed. After the revolution the subiect came up from time to time to the consideration of the governing powers, and new hospitals were erected, and great improvements made in the old ones. At the beginning of this century, they were placed under the direction of a general administration. All the civil hospitals and the different institutions connected with them, are under the control of an administrative committee. The regulations of the hospitals are nearly the same as they are in London and New York. In cases of severe wounds, persons are admitted into the hospitals without any order, by simply presenting themselves at the doors. Medical advice is given at some of the hospitals on certain days to poor persons. The hospitals of Paris are of three kinds; the general, open to all complaints for which a special hospital is not provided; the special hospitals, for the treatment of special diseases; and the alms-houses. The hospitals support more than twelve thousand aged men and women, receive more than eighty thousand patients, and have constantly under treatment six thousand persons.

Among the hospitals I may mention Bricètre, situated on the road to Fontainbleau. It is upon very high ground, and is the healthiest of all the hospitals from its position and arrangements. It is used as an asylum for poor old men, and for male lunatics. The old men have every encouragement to work, for they receive pay for their labor, slight, of course, and the money is devoted to giving them better food and clothes than the usual hospital allowance, which is some soup, one pound and a quarter of bread, four ounces of meat, vegetables, cheese, and a pint of wine each day. When seventy years old, the quantity of wine is doubled, and when a person has been thirty years an inmate of the house, the quantity of everything is doubled. Three thousand beds are made up for the indigent, and eight hundred for lunatics. The latter, of course, occupies a distinct part of the building.

There are two hospitals appropriated entirely to the use of men who have no hope of immediate cure, and are troubled with chronic ailments. The buildings are large and airy, and will accommodate four or five hundred.

The hospital of St. Louis, in Rue des Recollets, is very large, containing eight hundred beds. It is used for the special treatment of scrofula and cutaneous diseases. Persons able to pay, do so, but the poor are received without. It has very spacious bath accommodations, and it is estimated that as many as one hundred and forty thousand baths have been served in the establishment in the course of a year. The baths are in two large rooms, each containing fifty baths. The water is conducted to them in pipes, and every variety of mineral and sulphurous bath is given, as well as vapor and all kinds of water baths. The institution is very well managed, its work being all done within its walls, and so far is this principle carried, that the leeches needed for the diseased are cultivated in an artificial pond upon the premises.

In the Rue de Sevres is a hospital for incurable women It will accommodate six hundred women and seventy children. There are a few pictures in this establishment which are worth noticing. The Annunciation, the Flight into Egypt, and a Guardian Angel, possess great beauty.

The Louecine Hospital is for the reception of all females suffering with syphilitic diseases. It makes up three hundred beds, fifty of which are for children. The number of persons treated in Paris is more than two thousand every year, and the mortality is very slight.

Medical men dislike this hospital, for the diseases are such as to render their duties very unpleasant, but to in sure proper attendance, a regulation exists that every physician before making an application for a place in any of the hospitals, shall serve in the Louecine.

The Rouchefoucald Hospital is principally for the reception of old and worn-out servants, and is of course not kept up by state funds, though it is overseen by the government. Persons who enter the institution pay a sum of money, and are entitled to a room, fire, and food, so long as they live, and some enter even as young as the age of twenty. There is another establishment in Paris where only the middling classes are received, and who pay for the attention they receive. Single men who have no homes of their own, when attacked by violent diseases, can by paying a moderate sum enter this institution and be well cared for.

I cannot even mention a tenth part of the hospitals or charitable institutions of Paris, and will only allude to one or two more which are a little peculiar. There are, for example, *nurseries*, where poor women who must leave home for work in factories or similar places, can in the morning leave their babies, return occasionally to nurse them, and take them away at night. If a child is weaned, it has a little basket of his own. A very small sum of money is paid for this care, and as the nurseries have the best of medical attention, some mothers bring them for that purpose alone. There are public soup establishments to which any person with a soup-ticket can go and demand food. The tickets are dispensed with some care to persons in needy circumstances. In each of the twelve arrondissements of Paris there is a bureau for the relief of poor women having large families. When proper representations are made by such females struggling to keep from the alms-house, an allowance is made of bread, firing, meat, and clothing, and sometimes money is given. There are sometimes as many as thirty thousand dependent in this manner for a part of their income upon the state. Hence, bureaus are excellent institutions, inasmuch as prevention is always easier than cure. To save struggling families from the humiliation of a complete downfall to the poor-house, small weekly allowances are made, and in such a way that their pride need not be touched, for it is often done with such secrecy that even the intimate friends of the recipients are unaware of the relation existing between them and the state. Such an arrangement as this is needed in all the great cities of the world. London suffers from the want of it. In some places the parish authorities are at liberty to make grants to poor families, but it is nowhere done with such a system and with such a delicacy as in Paris.

Another of the charitable institutions of Paris lends money upon movable effects, the interest charged being very low. This is an excellent provision for emergencies in the lives of poor persons. There are at least a million and a half of articles pledged at this institution yearly, and its receipts are from twenty-six to twenty-eight millions a year. In winters of famine the public are sometimes allowed to pledge property without paying any interest upon it when redeemed. The Mont de Pietie, is the name of this institution, and it has branches all over Paris, and has in its employ, as clerks and otherwise, three hundred persons.

There are savings' banks in Paris specially adapted to the wants of the poor, and to encourage in them the habit of accumulating property, though in very small sums. A deposit of one franc is received, and one person cannot hold but two thousand francs at one time in one bank of the kind. This institution, however, is not superior to those of its kind in many other countries.

LA MORGUE.

On the southern side of Isle la Cité, there is a small stone building which is certainly one of the "sights" of Paris. I saw it one day when I had been to look at Notre Dame, and was on my way home. I was filled with admiration of the magnificence of the great city, for with Notre Dame and the Louvre in sight, I could not easily entertain other sentiments. A little building arrested my attention, and I saw quite a crowd of persons standing in front of it. It was *La Morgue.* I entered it, not that I have a penchant for horrors, but to see a sight strangely contrasting with all I had heretofore seen in Paris. It was a long, low interior, and one end of the room was fenced off from the rest, and in it a row of dead bodies was arranged against the wall. Jets of water were playing constantly upon them, and upon hooks the garments of the deceased were hung. The use of *La Morgue* is to exhibit, for twenty-four hours, the dead bodies which are found in the streets and the river. If no friend in this time recognizes and claims the body, it is buried. There were five bodies when I was there—four men and one woman. The men were evidently suicides and the women was probably murdered, as there were marks of violence

LE PONT-NEUF.

upon her body, which could not have been self-inflicted. There are several hundred persons exhibited in La Morgue in the course of a year, and they tell strange stories of the misery and crime which abound in the finest city in the world. The majority of the bodies which are found, are suicides, but many are those of persons who have been murdered. The French commit suicide for reasons which appear frivolous to the American or Englishman. The loss of a favorite mistress, an unsuccessful love-intrigue, the bursting of a bubble of speculation, and sometimes a mere trifle is enough to induce self-destruction. Sometimes a man and his mistress, or a whole family shut themselves up in a room with burning charcoal, which is a favorite method of committing suicide. A great many bodies are fished out of the Seine, for it is very easy for a poor and wretched man or woman to leap into it in the darkness of night. The next day the body lies for recognition in La Morgue, and if no good friend claims it it is borne by careless hands to a pauper burial.

I crossed the Seine by the Pont Neuf—a fine bridge, completed in 1604 by Henry IV. Near the center of it, standing upon a platform and pedestal of white marble, is a splendid bronze statue of Henry IV. upon horseback. The height of the statue is fourteen feet, and its cost, somewhat above sixty thousand dollars, was defrayed by public subscription in 1818.

The Place Vendome, too, lay in my path, so called from having been the site of a hotel belonging to the Duke de Vendome, illegitimate son of Henry IV. and Gabrielle d'Estrees. The Place is now ornamented by a magnificent pillar, erected by Napoleon in honor of his German campaign.

I passed also the beautiful Fountain des Innocents, whose sculptor, the celebrated Jean Goujon was shot during the massacre of St. Bartholomew, while working at one of the figures.

Fontaine des Innocents.

NAPOLEON AND EUGENIA.

On my second visit to Paris, I found that many changes had taken place, and some of them striking ones. It was especially true of the architectural condition of Paris. In the years which elapsed between my visits, the Louvre had assumed a new appearance, and was now connected with the Tuilleries Palace. Other changes of a similar character had occurred.

When I was first in Paris, Louis Napoleon was president,

COLUMN DE PLACE VENDOME.

but he was preparing for the empire, and there was in reality no more liberty in France than now, and in many respects a residence in Paris was then more uncomfortable than at present. Everybody was expecting a change, and Louis Napoleon, as president, was actually more despotic in little things than he is as emperor. He was then ready to hunt down any man against whom a suspicion could lie, while now his rule is, after a manner, established. He has as fair prospects to remain emperor of France till he dies, for aught that I can see, as any European monarch has of retaining his throne.

When I entered Paris, under the presidency, I was more closely watched than under the empire. As an American, from a republic, I was, perhaps, naturally an object of suspicion to the spies of a man who was planning a *coup d'etat;* at any rate I was tracked everywhere I stirred, by the police, while on my last visit I experienced nothing of the sort.

The people of Paris are divided into many classes in politics—some are the friends of Louis Napoleon, while others are his enemies. But he has few distinguished friends in Paris. The shop-keepers are pleased with the pomp and magnificence of his court, for it gives them custom and money. Many of the wealthy business men desire him to live and rule because they want a stable government, and they deprecate above all things else, change. They are more for money, as we may expect, than for freedom. Then there are the partisans of the Orleans and Bourbon families, who fear the republicans and accept Napoleon as a temporary ruler, and who much prefer him to anarchy. So that there is a strong body of men in Paris and in France—a majority of the people—whc upon the whole prefer that the rule of a man they all dislike should be perpetuated for years to come.

And there is something in the character of Louis Napoleon which excites admiration. He is intensely selfish, but he is a very capable man. He understands the French people thoroughly, and rules them shrewdly. He is one of the ablest statesmen in Europe, and the world knows that he lead England in the late war with Russia. Yet he possesses some ridiculous qualities, as his conduct previous to his last entrance into France shows. He relies upon his destiny in the blindest manner, and is not possessed of genuine courage of the highest character. He is so reckless that he will never flinch from the prosecution of any of his schemes, either from personal danger or the dread of shedding human blood. He seems to have no heart, and his countenance is like adamant, for it gives no clue to the thoughts which fill his brain. He is certainly a very remarkable character and one worth studying. His early history is laughable. His various descents upon France were too ridiculous for laughter, and they only excited the pity of the world. His private conduct, too, was such as to disgust moral people. There seems to have come over the man a great change about the time of the Louis Phillippe revolution. I well remember that in the spring of 1848 I saw him parading one of the streets of London, arm-in-arm with a son of Sir Robert Peel, both sworn in as special constables to put down the chartists should they attempt a riot. It was, on that memorable first of April, quite fashionable for members of the best families to be sworn in as special constables to preserve order, and Louis Napoleon who was living with his mistress and children in London, had so far put away the democratic opinions which he once held, that he was ready and eager to show where his sympathies were in the Chartist agitation.

That Louis Napoleon was very shrewd in entering France, and seating himself in the presidential chair, no one will deny, but it is equally true that in violating his oath and shooting down the people of Paris as he did, that he might gain a throne, he also proved himself to be a great villain. The mere fact that he was successful will not atone for perjury and murder with people of common morality. But aside from these atrocities, his shameful censorship of the press, and conduct toward some of the noblest men of France, he has acted for the best interests of the country. He has understood the wants of the people, and his decrees and provisions have met the wishes of the nation. France has not had the material prosperity for many years that she has at this time. But the press is dumb. Literature is in a sickly condition. Many of the first men of France are either in exile or are silent at home. It is astonishing to see how few of the really eminent men of France are the friends of Louis Napoleon. Lamartine does not like him; Eugene Sue was his enemy; the same is true in a modified sense of Alexander Dumas; George Sand dislikes him; Arago while living did the same; and Jules Janin the brilliant critic is no friend of the administration. Victor Hugo, Ledru Rollin, Louis Blanc, and a score of other brilliant men are in exile, and of course hate the man who exiled them. It is certainly one of the most singular facts of modern history that Louis Napoleon has few friends, yet is firmly seated upon his throne. His enemies are so divided, and so hate anarchy, that they all unite in keeping him where he is. But Paris laughs in its sleeve at all the baptismal splendors over the prince and the sober provisions for the regency made by the emperor. No one that I could find has the faintest expectation that the baby-boy will rule France, or sit upon a throne. When the emperor is shot or dies a violent death, then chaos will come, or something better, but not Napoleon IV. I am confident that this is the universal sentiment, at least throughout Paris, if not over France. I have asked many a Frenchman his opinion, and the same reply has been given by republican and monarchist. This is one secret of Napoleon's strength. It is thought that with his death great changes must come, and very likely confusion and bloodshed. No one believes in a Napoleon succession, and therefore all bear his despotism with equanimity. Those who hate him say his rule will not last forever, while those who wish to advance their own political interests through other royal families, bide their time.

It is possible that Louis Napoleon will live many years yet, or at least die a natural death, but there are those who have a reputation for shrewdness who do not believe it. They think that as he has taken the sword so he will perish by the sword, or in other words that a bullet will one day end his life. It would not be strange, for he has many bitter enemies, and there would be poetic justice in such a fate, to say the least.

The empress is quite popular in France, but not so much so as the journalists and letter-writers would make out. She is exceedingly handsome, and this fact goes a great way with the Parisians. Her conduct since her marriage has been irreproachable, which should always be mentioned to her credit. But that she is naturally a very lovely woman, gentle, and filled with all the virtues, few who know her early history will believe. She is, like the emperor, shrewd, and acts her part well. She is certainly equal to her position, and in goodness is satisfactory tc the French people. It has been thought by many that if Louis Napoleon had married a Frenchwoman it would have better satisfied the people, but this is by no means certain.

The emperor and empress seem to live together happily, or at least rumor hath nothing to the contrary; and he would be a brute not to be satisfied with the woman who has presented him with what he desired above everything else—a male heir.

Portraits of the empress abound in all the shops and in private houses. Her great beauty is the passport to the French heart. It is not of the dashing, bold style, but is delicate and refined. Louis Napoleon has in his provisions for the prince calculated largely upon the popularity of the empress, in case of his own death.

He confides the boy-prince to the Empress Eugenia, and thinks her popularity is such, and the gallantry of the people so great, that they will gather round her in the day of trouble. But though the French are a gallant people they estimate some things higher than politeness or gallantry. There is no loyalty in France. The only feeling which approaches to it is the veneration which is felt in some of the provinces for the elder Napoleon. But that sentiment of loyalty which is felt in all ranks and circles in England is unknown to France. Who carries in his bosom that sentiment towards the man who procured his throne by perjury? Not a single Frenchman. Many admire his intellect, his daring, and many others accept his rule with pleasure, but nobody has the feeling of loyalty toward him. It has died out in France, and I must confess that this is a good sign. While it is true, France cannot really *like* a monarchical despotism, though she may for a long time endure it.

THE BAPTISM OF THE PRINCE.

The 14th of June was a great day in Paris, for it witnessed the baptism of the prince and heir to the French throne. It was not because Paris was or is devoted to the present Napoleonic dynasty, not because the birth of an heir to Louis Napoleon was or is regarded with any remarkable enthusiasm, but simply for this reason: Paris loves gayety, and above all things is fond of a public *fête*.

Louis Napoleon well knew how to make the day memorable. All that was wanting was money—a prodigious pile of Napoleons. With this he could easily make a pageant.

The young baby-prince was baptized in the ancient church of Notre Dame, which was fitted up in a magnificent style expressly for the occasion. On each side of the grand nave, between the main columns hung with gold and crimson drapery, a series of seats were erected, also covered with crimson velvet and gold decorations. Around the altar seats were erected for the legislative body, the senate, the diplomatic corps, and officers of state. Above these, galleries were formed, hung with drapery, for the occupation of ladies. The appearance of the interior was grand in the extreme, but it needed the splendid concourse soon to be present, to add a wonderful beauty to it.

A few minutes past six o'clock a burst of drums announced the arrival of the grand cortege in the ancient city, and the archbishop of Paris, with his assistants, went to the door or grand entrance of Notre Dame, to receive Napoleon and Eugenia. The princes and princesses had already alighted, and were ready with the clergy to receive the emperor and empress.

The procession was in something like the following order: First came the cross, followed by the archbishop and his vicar-generals. Next came the military officers of the imperial household. Then what are called the honors of the imperial infant, as follows—the wax taper of the Countess Montebello; the crimson cloth of Baroness Malaret; and the salt-cellar of the Marquess Tourmanbourg. Then came the sponsorial honors. These ladies all walked in couples, and were dressed in blue, vailed in white transparent drapery. The grand duchess of Baden and Prince Oscar of Sweden immediately preceded the prince.

The royal babe wore a long ermine mantile, and was carried by a gouvernante with two assistants, one on each side of her. The nurse followed, clad in her native costume—that of Burgundy. Marshals Canrobert and Bosquet followed the infant, and their majesties next appeared under a moving canopy.

The cardinal-legate had appeared and been welcomed before, and took his seat upon a throne erected expressly for him. Immediately in front of the altar there was erected a crimson platform, on which two crimson chairs were placed for the accommodation of Napoleon and Eugenia. Far above there was a crimson canopy lined with white, and spotted with golden bees.

Napoleon advanced up the aisle on the right of Eugenia, and a pace in advance. He did not offer her his arm, as that is considered improper in a church, according to Parisian notions of propriety. Eugenia was dressed in a light blue, covered with an exquisite lace, and she was covered with dazzling diamonds. The jewels she wore were worth nearly five millions of dollars. The blue color worn by nearly all the ladies present, was considered the appropriate color for the ruder sex of the baby. Napoleon wore the uniform of a general officer, but with white knee pants and silk stockings. He wore several orders.

Everything being ready, the cardinal-legate left his throne, went to the foot of the altar, and commenced the *Veni Creator*, which was taken up and executed by the fine orchestra. The music was inexpressibly grand. When it was concluded the masters of ceremonies saluted the altar and their majesties, and then waited upon the legate, who at once catechised the sponsors. He then conducted the royal babe to the font, holding the baptismal robe. Napoleon and Eugenia ascended the throne. The duchess of Baden, representing the god-mother, advanced to the font. The god-father was the pope, represented by the legate. The baptism was then proceeded with.

When the rite was performed, the gouvernante presented the babe to its mother, who at once handed it over to its royal papa, who held it up to the crowd of gazers, and then the cries of "*Vive le Prince Imperial!*" came near destroying the solid masonry of Notre Dame. After this the royal pair soon took their departure, though there were many ceremonies after they had left.

A magnificent banquet was at once given to their majesties by the city of Paris, in the *Hotel de Ville*, and it was probably one of the most luxurious the world ever witnessed. All the male guests were in official costume, and the ladies were dressed with great richness.

The next day—Sunday—was the great day for outdoor *fêtes*, though this was widely celebrated. The day was given up to all kinds of enjoyment, and the emperor gave immense sums to make the people good-humored and enthusiastic. There was a display of fire-works in the evening rarely equaled, and probably never surpassed. The theaters were all open, free to all who came, and could gain entrance. In the course of the day more than three hundred balloons were sent up, laden with confectionary and things to tickle the palate, and showered down upon the multitude. The whole of Paris was gay, and the stranger had a fine sample of a grand Parisian *fête*, and Sabbath—both in one!

CHAPTER XI.

THE FATHER OF FRENCH TRAGEDY—THE JESTER—THE DRAMATIST.

MEN OF THE PAST.

During my residence in Paris I became very much interested in the history of the great men of France, not only in the present day, but in past years. I was not so well acquainted with the great French masters in literature, especially of the past, as with the great men of English history. I believe this to be the fact with most Americans. I soon found that to know France, to know Paris to-day, I needed to have by heart the history of her heroes of to-day and yesterday, and especially of those great men who made Paris their home and final resting-place. The influence of these men over the minds, manners, and even the morals of the people of Paris, is still very great. Nowhere is genius more praised, or adored with a greater devotion, than in Paris. Rank must there doff its hat to genius, which is the case in no other country but the American republic. It will then not be out of place for me to sketch a very few of the most brilliant men who in the years which have fled away lighted with their smiles the saloons of Paris. I will commence with

THE FATHER OF FRENCH TRAGEDY.

In the Rue d'Argenteuil, number 18, there is a small quiet house, in which Corneille, the father of French tragedy, breathed his last. It has a black marble slab in front, and a bust in the yard with the following inscription:

"*Je ne dois qu'á moi seul toute ma renommeé.*"

The great man lies buried in the beautiful church of St. Roch, where a tablet is erected to his memory.

Corneille was the son of Pierre Corneille, master of forests and waters in the viscounty of Rouen. His mother was of noble descent, but the couple were somewhat poor. The dramatist was born in 1606, and early became a pupil of the Jesuits of Rouen. He was educated for the law, but had no taste for that profession, and although he attempted to practice it he was unsuccessful. It was well for France that such was the fact, for had it been otherwise, she would have lost one of her most brilliant names.

When Corneille entered upon life, there was no theater in France, though there were exhibitions of various kinds. At last a few wretched plays were written by inferior men, and they were acted upon the stage by inferior actors. Corneille, while vainly endeavoring to win success at the bar, was incited to write a comedy, and produced one under the title of "*Melite.*" The plot was suggested by an incident in his own life. A friend of his was very much in love with a lady, and introduced him to her, that he might, after beholding her charms, indite a sonnet to her in the name of his friend. The poet found great favor in the eyes of the lady, and the original lover was cast into the shade. This incident was the reason why Corneille wrote "*Melite.*" The success of the piece was very great, a new company of players was established in Paris, and at that time it was fully equal to any comedy which had been written in the French language, though it reads dull enough at the present day. The poet traveled up to Paris to witness his play upon the stage, and was so well pleased with its reception, that he went on writing plays. They were without merit, however. He had not yet struck the key-note of his after greatness.

With four other authors, Corneille was appointed to correct the plays of Richelieu. Parties quickly sprung into existence in the *salons* of Paris. Some of them espoused the cause of Corneille—others openly traduced his plays and were his enemies. He had the independence to correct one of Richelieu's plays without the consent of his comrades, and Richelieu reprimanded him for it. He became disgusted and left Paris for Rouen. He was quite willing, too, to return to the lady who had inspired his sonnet. She was very beautiful, and he continued to love her until his death, and this may be said to be the only lasting passion of his life.

The poet was not much of a scholar, though well informed. He next wrote a tragedy entitled "*Media*," and then another comedy called "*The Illusion.*" But he had not yet hit upon the note of success. Soon after, when about thirty years of age, he commenced the study of the Spanish language.

An Italian secretary of the queen counseled him to this course, and advised him to read the "*Cid*" of de Castro, with an idea of making it a subject for a drama. Corneille followed his advice, and produced a tragedy which roused all France to enthusiasm. Paris was one prolonged storm of applause, and when one praised an object, he said "It is fine as the *Cid!*" The play was translated into the different languages of all the civilized nations. Fontenelle says: "I knew two men, a soldier and a mathematician, who had never heard of any other play that had ever been written, but the name of Cid had penetrated even the barbarous state in which they lived."

The dramatist had enemies—no man can quickly achieve renown without making them—and some of them were exceedingly bitter in their attacks upon him. Richelieu, the cardinal, was excessively annoyed that the man he had reprimanded should have achieved success, and the French Academy of Criticism, which was deeply under his influence, after discussions decided somewhat against "The Cid." This suited the cardinal, but the poet kept a wise silence, making no reply.

The next effort of Corneille was that resulting in the tragedy of "*Horace*," which was a master-piece, and was received with unbounded applause. He surpassed this effort, however, in his next piece, called "*Cinna*." After this—which many consider his best drama—came "*Polyeceute*," a beautiful piece. In it the christian virtues are illustrated, and when read before a conclave of learned men, they deputied Voiture to the poet, to induce him, if possible, to withdraw it, for the christianity in it the people would not endure. But the play went to the people without amendment, and so beautiful was its character, and so delightful the acting, that it carried away the hearts of the listeners.

Corneille now tried again to write comedy, but did not succeed so well as in tragedy. He triumphed, however, over a rival, and that to him was something, though the play is an inferior one. From this time the poet wrote no better, but in truth worse and worse. He did not fail to write beautiful scenes, but failed in selecting good subjects. He established himself in Paris, and could do so with comfort, for the king bestowed a pension upon him. Before this he had resided at Rouen, running up to Paris quite often. In 1642 he was elected a member of the French Academy. He was never a courtier, and was not fitted to shine in gay Parisian circles. His tastes were very simple, and he was in his manners like a rustic. To see him in a drawing-room you would not think the man a genius, nor even a bright specimen of his kind. Some of his friends remonstrated with him, and tried to rouse him from his sluggishness in society. He always replied, "I am not the less Pierre Corneille."

La Bruyere says of him, "He is simple and timid; tiresome in conversation—using one word for another—he knows not how to recite his own verses." It is strange that he came to Paris, for he loved the country better, and many attribute the remove to his brother, who was also winning success as a dramatist.

It had been well if after this Corneille had been content to write no more plays, for every one he now produced only proved that his genius had decayed. The old cunning was gone. A young rival sprung up, the graceful Racine, and for awhile the old favorite was forgotten, or laughed at.

Racine took a line from one of his pieces and used it in such a manner as to excite laughter. Corneille said: "It ill becomes a young man to make game of other people's verses." Unfortunately he was tempted into a duel with Racine. The latter triumphed as a writer for the time, and Corneille stopped his pen, as he should have done a long time before. But often he had the pleasure of seeing some of his best pieces enacted upon the stage, and they always excited great enthusiasm. He also knew that the refined and critical loved his best plays—the better the more they read them.

The conduct of the poet through his whole life was, in

the main, such as to excite great admiration in after generations. He was no sycophant in that age of fawning courtiers. He was simple and manly. He was always melancholy and cared little for the vanities of life. Though poor in early life, he cared but little about money. The king gave him a pension of two thousand francs, which at that time was a good income. He was generous and died utterly poor. One evening when age had bowed his form he entered a Paris theater. The great *Condé* was present, and prince and people as one man rose in honor of the great dramatist. He died in his seventy-ninth year, and Racine pronounced a high eulogy upon him, before the academy. Such was its beauty that the king caused it to be recited before him. In it he extolled the genius of the man who had at one time been his rival, and he taught his children to revere his memory.

In France, much more in Paris, the name of Corneille is to-day half sacred. The house he lived and died in has many visitors, and to his tomb many a pilgrim comes. And it is not strange that Parisians adore him, for he was the father of comedy as well as tragedy. It was his plays that caused the erection of commodious theaters. His plays have continued to hold their place in the affections of the nation, and he is reverenced more to-day than he was while living. The foreigner cannot understand fully the character of modern French dramatists, and that of their works, without knowing something of Corneille, nor can he wander long among the streets of Paris, without becoming aware of the estimation in which he is held at the present time by the intelligent classes.

THE GREAT JESTER.

Rabelais was born in 1483. He was a learned scholar, a physician, and a philosopher. He was called "the great jester of France," by Lord Bacon. Many buffooneries are ascribed to him unjustly, and he was a greater man than certain modern writers make him out to be.

His place of birth was Chinòn, a little town of Touraine. His father was a man of humble means. He received his early education in a convent near his home. His progress was very slow and he was removed to another. He promised poorly for future distinction, but at the second convent he was fortunate in making the acquaintance of Du Ballay who afterward became a bishop and cardinal, and whose friendship he retained to the day of his death.

He was again removed to another convent, where he applied himself to the cultivation of his talents. There was, however, no library in the place. Rabelais soon took to preaching, and with the money he was paid for it, he purchased books. His brother monks hated him for his eloquence in preaching, and for his evident learning. He was persecuted by these men and suffered a great deal, principally because he knew Greek. For some alleged slight offered against the rules of the convent, they wreaked their vengeance upon him by condemning him to the prison cell, and to a diet of bread and water. They also applied their hempen cords thoroughly, and this course of treatment soon reduced Rabelais to a very weak condition. His friends were by this time powerful and they obtained his release, and a license from the Pope for him to pass from this convent to another. But he was thoroughly disgusted with convent life, and fled from it, wandering over the provinces as a secular priest. He next gave up this employment altogether, and took to the study of medicine. He went through the different steps of promotion and was made a professor. He delivered medical lectures, and a volume of his—an edition of Hippocrates —was long held in high estimation by the medical faculty of France.

A medical college of Montpellier had been deprived for some reason of its privileges, and Rabelais was deputed to Chancelor Duprat to solicit a restoration of them. The story is told—to illustrate his learning—that when he knocked at the chancellor's house he addressed the person who came to the door in Latin, who could not understand that language; a man shortly presented himself who could, and Rabelais addressed him in Greek. Another man was sent for, and he was addressed in Hebrew, and so on. The singularity of the circumstance arrested the attention of the chancelor, and Rabelais was at once invited to his presence. He succeeded in restoring the lost honors to the college, and such was the enthusiasm of the students that ever after, when taking degrees, they wore Rabelais scarlet gowns. This usage continued till the revolution.

Rabelais now went to Lyons, and still later to Rome as the physician to Du Ballay, who was ambassador at that court. Some writers claim that he went as buffoon instead of physician, but this is unsupported by evidence. Many stories are told of his buffooneries at the court of Rome, but unquestionably the majority were entirely untrue. One story told, however, is good enough to be true. The pope expressed his willingness to grant Rabelais a favor. The wit replied that if such was the fact, he begged his holiness to excommunicate him. The pope wished to know the reason. The wit replied that some very honest gentlemen of his acquaintance in Touraine had been burned, and finding it a common saying in Italy when a fagot would not burn "that it had been excommunicated by the pope's own mouth," he wished to be rendered incombustible by the same process. It is asserted that Rabelais offended the pope by his buffooneries, but the assertion can scarcely be believed. When he had resided for a time in Rome, Rabelais went to Lyons, then returned to the holy city, and after a second visit went to Paris, where he entered the family of Cardinal du Bellay, who had also returned from Rome. He confided to Rabelais the government of his household, and persuaded the pope to secularize the abbey of St. Maurdes-Fosses, and conferred it upon the wit. He next bestowed upon him the cure of Meudon, which he retained while he lived.

One of the first of Rabelais' books was entitled "*Lives of the great Giant Garagantua and his Son Pantagruel.*" To it he owes a great deal of his reputation and popularity. It created a vast deal of talk, and was both highly praised and bitterly attacked. The champions of the church criticised his book with great severity. Calvin the reformer also wrote against it with much earnestness. The Sorbonne attacked it for teaching heresy and atheism, and it was condemned by the court of parliament.

The subjects held up for ridicule were the vices of the popes, the avarice of the prelates, and the universal debaucheries of the monastic orders. It was a wonderful book for the times, and it required great courage in Rabelais to venture upon its publication. He would have lost position, and perhaps his liberty, had it not been for the monarch Francis I., who sent for the volume, read it, and declared it to be innocent and good reading, and protected the author. The sentence against the book amounted to nothing after this, and it was everywhere read and admired. Rabelais was set down as the first wit and scholar of his age.

The character of the book we have noticed cannot be defended. Its irreverent use of scripture quotations, and loose wit, are not to be overlooked, but there was no advocacy of atheism in it. Indeed we must look upon Rabelais as acting the part of a reformer. If he had sought simply popularity and the favor of the court and church, he would certainly not have written a book which is a scathing attack upon pope, prelate, and monk. The book is full of dirty expressions—but the age was a very impure one, and we should not judge him too severely. He was a Frenchman, and French wit in all ages has taken great liberties with decency.

Among the other books which Rabelais wrote, we may mention "*Several Almanacs*," "*The Powers of Chevalier de Langery*," "*Letters from Italy*," "*The Philosophical Cream*," etc. etc. His greatest book, which we have mentioned, went through a great number of editions and had a tremendous sale. It was republished in several foreign states.

Rabelais was a scholar, for he knew well fourteen languages, and wrote with facility Greek, Latin, and Italian. He was a good physician, an accomplished naturalist, a correct mathematician, an astronomer, an architect, a painter, a musician, and last of all, a wit and philosopher. He was a good pastor over the parishioners of Meudon, and acted as physician to their bodies as well as souls.

There are idle tales to the effect that he made his will as follows: "I have nothing—I owe much—I leave the rest to the poor." And also that he sent a message as fol lows, to Cardinal du Ballay. "Tell the cardinal I am going to try the great 'perhaps'—you are a fool—draw the curtain—the farce is done." These were fictions invented by the very pious Catholics, who hated him for his satires upon the church.

Rabelais must have been a great man. Even his learning alone would have made him the most distinguished man in France at the time he lived. Those who hated him have tried to cover his memory with shame, and have represented him as merely a buffoon, but such was not the truth. He did often descend to buffooneries and to almost obscene sayings, and these things have had their influence upon France, and have contributed to make the French people what they are to-day—a nation of professed Catholics, but really a nation of infidels and atheists. But Rabelais was more than a wit. He was a public benefactor. He improved medical science, and was as much a reformer in his laughable attacks upon the fat and lazy monks, as was Calvin himself.

Rabelais died at the age of seventy, and was buried in the churchyard of St. Paul, Rue des Jardins, at the foot of a beautiful tree which was preserved in his memory. No monument was ever placed over his grave, but he did not need one to perpetuate his memory.

THE DRAMATIST.

One of the men of the past who exerted and still exerts a wide influence over French literature, is Racine. He was born in 1639, in the small town Ferte-Milon, in Valois. The parents died while he was in infancy, and he and a sister, their only children, were left orphans in the care of their maternal grandfather. This sister remained in Ferte-Milon during her life, which was not long. Racine was not happy while young, and being neglected by his grandparents felt it keenly. He was a scholar at Beauvais, and attached himself to one of the political parties which at that time always sprang up in schools and colleges. He was in one of their contests wounded upon his forehead, and bore the scar through life.

Racine was transferred from Beauvais to the school of the convent of Port Royal, and the Jesuits noticing his natural quickness, bestowed careful attention upon his education. He was so wretchedly poor that he could not buy copies of the classics, and he was obliged to use those owned by others, and which were much inferior to copies he could have purchased had he possessed money. He was early struck with the beauty of the Greek writers—and more especially the Greek tragedians. He wandered in the woods with Sophocles and Euripides in his hands, and many years after could recite their chief plays from memory. He got hold of the Greek romance of Theogines and Chariclea, but the priests would not tolerate such reading and committed the volume to the flames. He got another copy and it shared the same fate. He concluded to purchase another, kept it till he learned it by heart, and then took it to the priests and told them they might have that also.

At Port Royal Racine was happy. He was a gentle-hearted boy and his masters loved him. He early began to compose verses and showed an intense love of poetry. At nineteen he left Port Royal for the college of Harcour, at Paris. When he was twenty-one Louis XIV. was married, and invited every versifier in the kingdom to write in honor of the occasion. Racine was an obscure student and was unknown as a poet. He wrote a poem on the marriage, and it was shown to M. Chapelain, who was the poetical critic of Paris at that time. He thought it showed a good deal of promise and suggested a few alterations. It was carried to the patron of the critic, who sent him a hundred louis from the king, and a pension of six hundred livres. The poet's friends were anxious that he should choose a profession, and that of the bar was strongly urged upon him. He objected. An uncle who had a benefice at Uzes, wished to resign it to his nephew. Racine concluded to visit his uncle in the provinces. He remained for some time there, but he found there was little hope of advancement and grew restless. The scenery around him was magnificent, yet, though he was a poet, he had no eye for the grand and impressive in scenery. He was too much of a Parisian for that. A Parisian is all art—and cares nothing for nature. He prefers fine buildings and paintings to fields, mountains, and majestic rivers.

Racine wrote a poem entitled "*The Bath of Venus*," and began a play upon the Greek one of Theogines and Chariclea, which had delighted him so much when he was young. He returned to Paris somewhat discouraged, after an abscence of only three months. Here, through the rivalry of two play-writers, he was persuaded to write very hastily a new play. He consented, and produced one which was well received by the Parisians. It did not do justice to his powers, however, and he soon after wrote "*Alexandre*," which was an advance upon the previous performance. He was unacquainted with the English or Spanish drama, and had studied only the French of Corneille, and the Greek. He attempted the Greek drama, and of course found it very difficult to render dramas founded upon Grecian national subjects, and with Grecian manners, interesting to a Parisian audience. "*Alexandre*" was not successful upon the stage, but the best critics did not hesitate to award the premium of great dramatic genius to Racine, and he was encouraged to go on.

While the dramatist was writing "*Andromaque*," he was bitterly attacked by the leader of a sect of religionists for the wretched morality of his play. He felt the attack keenly, and that it was just, no American will deny, though Frenchmen will. The poet replied to the attack in a witty and satirical letter.

The "*Andromaque*" of Racine had a fine success, and one character was so full of passion and was so well represented upon the stage, that it cost the life of the actor who fell dead from excitement. Then followed in quick succession "*Brittonicus*" and "*Berenice*," which were also successful. His plays were full of intense passion and eloquence, and it would not give the reader a fair idea of their influence over the French, did we not admit that their representations of human life were such as to undermine the morality of those who listened to them. The plays of Racine have exerted a prodigious influence over the intelligent clases of Paris, and their wretched morality poisoned the nation. For my part, when I consider the literature of France—and no one can judge of a people without knowing its literature—I do not wonder that a very low morality exists throughout the country, but more especially in Paris. The great plays of past and modern times are saturated with licentiousness—the great romances of past and present years, are foul with impurities. Racine, living in an age of licentiousness, reflects it in his plays, and his plays are admired to-day in Paris, as of yore; hence it follows that those who go and see them acted must be somewhat affected by their immorality. Madame Rachel has made the characters of Racine familiar to all France, and has revived all his blemishes as well as beauties.

The poet met with much severe criticism after the representation of the last mentioned of his plays. Madame Sevigne was one of Corneille's warmest admirers, and did not join the company of Racine worshipers. A benefice was now given the poet, but soon after it was disputed by a priest; lawsuits began, and finally he relinquished it in disgust. Racine, Moliere, Boileau, and others were in the habit of meeting and having convivial suppers together, and on such occasions Racine projected new plays, and characters were often suggested to him by his fellow authors. In one of his after plays, which was not successful, he showed a talent for comedy far above mediocrity. It was once represented before the king, who laughed so hard that his courtiers were astonished.

Racine was elected member of the Academy in 1673, and made a very modest speech when the honor was conferred upon him. He brought out one after another, "*Bajazet*," "*Mithridates*," "*Phœdra*" and "*Iphigenia*," all of which had an excellent reception. The day

"*Phædra*" was brought out, another dramatist brought out a drama with the same title. He had powerful friends who went so far as to pack his theater, and buy boxes at the theater upon the stage of which Racine's play was to be enacted, and leave them empty. This incident shows us the fierceness of rivalry between authors at that time. To such an extent was the quarrel carried by the friends of the respective authors, that Racine, who was a very sensitive man, resolved to renounce the drama. His early religious education tended to strengthen his resolution. He soon became a severe and stern religionist, undergoing penances to expiate the guilt incurred for his life of sin. His confessor advised him to marry some woman of piety, to help him on in his good work, and he therefore married. The woman was Catherine de Romenet. She was of a higher position, and was wealthy. She knew nothing of the drama, was not fond of poetry, and was a very strict religious woman. She was sincere and affectionate, and wrought a wonderful change in Racine. Under her quiet tuition he became very narrow in his religious convictions, but quite happy in his mind. He brought up his children with the same views, and they all took monastic vows. His daughters were, one after another, given to the convent. He had seven children in all, and found it difficult to meet all his family expenses.

At this time he was made historiographer to the king, and witnessed many important battles. His life at court was very pleasant to him, and though he was a little too much inclined to be servile, yet he was generally an upright man. The story is told of him, that once when in the bosom of his little family, an attendant of the great duke came to invite him to dinner at the Hotel de Conde.

He sent back the reply, "I cannot go; I have returned

to my family after an absence of eight days; they have got a fine carp for me, and would be much disappointed if I did not share it with them."

Boileau and Racine were very intimate friends, and many anecdotes are related of them. Boileau had wit—Racine humor, and a natural turn for raillery. The contests of the two were often amusing. The king was much pleased with the dramatist, and gave him a suit of apartments in the palace, and the privilege of attending his parties. Madame de Maintenon made a great favorite of him. He could recite poetry freely, and was asked to declaim before a young princess. He found that she had been learning some of his own plays. One of the best of his plays was performed in the presence of Madame de Maintenon, who liked it so well that she beseeched him to write a play which should contain no offensive sentiments. Racine was in agony, for he feared to injure his reputation. His vow prevented his return to his old employment, yet he feared to refuse the request. He compromised the matter by dramatising the touching bible history of Esther. At court the play had a wonderful success, and the poet tried again upon the story of Alheliah of the house of Judah; and in "*Alhalie*" we have the best of all his dramas. Singular as it may seem, this play was not well received at court, and Racine felt mortified. Boileau told him, however, that posterity would declare it the best of all his plays, and he was right.

It was about this time that the dramatist received the keenest blow which he had experienced in his lifetime, and which broke his heart. Madame de Maintenon was his warm friend, and was extremely fond of his society. The country was at that time in great distress, and she conversed with the poet upon the subject. She was much pleased with his observations, and asked him to commit them to paper, promising that what he should write should be seen by no eye but her own. He complied with her request, and while she was one day reading his essay, the king suddenly entered, and casting his eye upon the paper, demanded the name of the author. Madame de Maintenon broke her promise, and gave the name of the writer. The king was very angry, and asked, "Does he think that he knows everything because he writes verses?"

Madame de Maintenon saw at once that the king was much displeased, and felt it to be her duty to inform the the poet, that he might stay away from court for awhile, until the monarch's anger died away. Racine was plunged into the deepest distress, and grew daily weak and ill. He wandered over the park of Versailles, hoping to accidentally meet Madame de Maintenon, for she did not dare to receive him publicly. He at length met her, and she promised that she would yet bring pleasanter days to the poet—that the cloud would soon pass away. He replied with great melancholy that no fair weather would return for him.

One day, while in his study, he was seized with a sudden illness, and was obliged to take at once to his bed. An abscess in his liver had closed, though this was not known at the time. His disease grew very painful, and he became more patient and resigned. As death drew near, his original sweetness of disposition came back to him, and his deep melancholy fled away. The nobles of the court gathered around his bedside, and the king sent to make inquiries as to his condition. He arranged all his pecuniary affairs. Boileau was with him, and when he bade him farewell, he said, "I look on it as a happiness that I die before you."

When the physicians had discovered the abscess in his liver, they resolved upon an operation, and he consented, though with no hope of saving his life. He said, "The physicians try to give me hope, and God could restore me; but the work of death is done." In three more days he expired, in his sixtieth year. Thus lived and died one of the most brilliant men in the history of France.

CHAPTER XII.

THE FABULIST—THE INFIDEL—THE COMIC WRITER

THE FABULIST.

La Fontaine, the fabulist, was buried by the side of Moliere, who died long before him. He was born July 8th, 1621, at Chateau Thierry. His father was keeper of the royal domains. While young, La Fontaine gave no promise of his after distinction. His teachers declared him to be a dunce. His father, who seems to have been an admirer of poetry, persuaded him to attempt to write verses, but he could not make a rhyme. Seeing at nineteen that he could not make a poet of his son, the old man resolved to make a priest of him. After eighteen months of trial the young man returned to society. His father then proposed that he should take the keepership of the royal domains, and marry Marie d'Hericart, the daughter of his friend. La Fontaine made no objection, though we have no evidence that he loved the girl. She was both beautiful and talented, however. The father still clung to the idea that his son could write poetry, and with a kind of prophetic instinct.

When La Fontaine was twenty-two, a French officer visited him, who was a great admirer of poetry, and who brought the poems of Malherbe. La Fontaine became excited by the poetry, or the passionate recitation, and for days did nothing but read and recite poetry. He commenced writing odes in imitation of Malherbe, and when his father beheld his first attempt, he cried for joy. The character of the poetry was certainly different from that which afterward gave him his fame. He soon discovered the secret of success. By studying the old authors, he improved his taste, and acquired a disrelish for French literature. He was very fond of the Italian authors, but not knowing Greek, he only read the Greek authors through translations made by others. He was exceedingly fond of Plato, and his favorite copy was entirely filled with annotations.

La Fontaine remained for several years at Thierry, indolent, except in his reading, and neglecting his business and his family. His "*Adonis*" was written at this time. His good nature and simplicity are well illustrated by an anecdote which is told of him. An officer was in the constant habit of visiting his house, and his friends told him that the reputation of Madame La Fontaine was compromised, and that nothing was left but for him to challenge the officer to a duel. Now the fabulist cared little for madame, and less for his own reputation in connection with hers; but he believed his friends, and so after a great effort shook off his indolence, and early one morning went to the officer, who was in bed, and demanded that he should rise at once and go out to mortal combat. The officer rose and followed him, and easily disarmed him. An explanation followed. The friends of La Fontaine had been joking him, and when the officer declared that he would never cross the threshold of Thierry again, La Fontaine told him that thenceforth he should come more frequently than ever.

But though Madame La Fontaine was guiltless in this affair, her character was by no means above reproach. She was giddy and thoughtless, and fond of the society of gentlemen, and made a poor wife for the poet. But she had an excuse. La Fontaine bestowed upon her no attention, deserted her for weeks together, and was guilty of amours with other women. He possessed a wretched memory, and was given to astonishing absences of mind. The duchess of Bouillon left him one morning walking in the open air, with a favorite book in his hand. At night he was still there, though it had been raining hard for some time.

His acquaintance with the duchess of Bouillon was of great service to him. Had it not been for her he would probably never have left Thierry. She was at that time in the country, being disgraced and exiled from court. She was gay, witty, and fond of poetry. Chancing to read some lines of La Fontaine, she sent for him, and at once saw his genius, and suggested that he should write tales and fables. When the duchess was allowed to return to Paris she took La Fontaine with her, and he was at once introduced into the most brilliant society. The duchess of Mazarin, sister to the duchess of Bouillon, was also his warm friend; and with the friendship of the two sisters he had no lack of attention. He became acquainted with Moliere, Boileau, and Racine, and was warmly attached to them until death invaded the circle.

The circles which La Fontaine frequented were amused by his great eccentricities. He was often seized with his absences of mind, and great sport was made of him. But Moliere was in the habit of saying at such times, "The good man will take a flight beyond them,"—a prediction which proved perfectly true, for the name of La Fontaine will live longer than that of any of his companions.

Boileau and Racine remonstrated with La Fontaine for

having separated from his wife. Simple as he was, he believed what they told him—that it was his duty to return to her. He very soon came back, and when he was asked why he came back so soon, he replied, "I did not see her!"

"How," they asked, "was she from home?"

"Yes," he replied; "she was gone to prayers, and the servant not knowing me, would not let me stay in the house until she returned."

The fabulist and his wife were so extravagant and careless in their habits, that in a very short time the property of La Fontaine was wasted away. Foquet, the minister, pensioned him, and he remembered him always after. When Foquet was banished, La Fontaine solicited his pardon, but the king was incapable of forgiving an enemy, and changed the sentence to solitary confinement for life. The succeeding minister took away La Fontaine's pension, as might have been expected.

In 1664 La Fontaine published his first collection of fables, and it gave him immediately the very highest rank as a fabulist. Shortly after, he published a tale entitled "*Psyche and Cupid.*" He was now without money and a home. The duchess of Orleans added him to her suite, and gave him a pension. She soon died, however, and he was again left homeless. A woman by the name of de la Sabliere now invited him to her house, and with her he lived the next twenty years. She was a woman of great refinement and taste, but was singularly situated. She lived apart from her husband, and had her lover. She gave parties which the most distinguished men in France attended, and La Fontaine was very happy while in her house. He was oppressed by no care or anxiety, and had nothing to do but to read and write when it suited him. He wrote several operas, and actually fell asleep during the first performance of one of them at the theater!

In 1683 he was elected a member of the French Academy. He had forgotten his old friends at Thierry, and indeed did not know his own son. He attended the funeral of a friend, one day, and ten days after it had so completely escaped his memory, that he called to visit the man. He was lionized, greatly to his displeasure. Attending one day at a dinner given by somebody who cared nothing for his genius, but wished the *eclat* that would result from entertaining a great man, La Fontaine talked little, eat very heartily, and when dinner was over, got his hat to go. The host remonstrated: "The distance is short—you will be too early," he said. "I'll take the longest road," replied La Fontaine.

After twenty years of easy existence, La Fontaine was suddenly deprived of his home. Madame de la Sabliere had been living all this time with her lover. He now deserted her. At the same time her husband was deserted by his mistress, which so affected him that he took poison and died. These events had so great an effect upon Madame de la Sabliere that she also died.

The duchess of Bouillon was now in England, and she invited La Fontaine to join her there; but he was now too old, and could not undertake such a journey. Madame d'Hevvart, the wife of a rich man, gave him an apartment in her house, where he remained during the rest of his days. He was now getting infirm, and the Jesuits turned their eyes toward him. He had thus far lived without a profession of religion, and a life of loose morality. The Jesuits cared little for his want of good morals, but in many of his books he had ridiculed the church and the clergy. It was important, therefore, to make him confess his sins. Father Poujet, a shrewd and subtle Jesuit, was sent to converse with him. In a very short time he contrived to insinuate himself into the confidence of the simple poet. He acknowledged, one after another, the truths of religion, and he was called on to make expiations and a public confession. He was easily persuaded to burn his operas, and to give up all the profits resulting from the sale of a volume of his worst tales; but he rebelled against public confession. Three doctors of the Sorbonne were sent to him, and they argued long and well, but to no purpose. An old man who was angered by their bull-dog pertinancy, said, "Don't torment him, my reverend fathers; it is not ill will in him, but stupidity, poor soul; and God Almighty will not have the heart to damn him for it.

That La Fontaine finally made some kind of a confession, there is little doubt; but that he made the shameful confession which Catholic writers declare he did, no one now believes. He was probably worn out with their entreaties, and came to a compromise with them.

He added nothing to his reputation after this, but rather detracted from it. He lived very quietly and devotedly, and died in 1695, in the seventy-fourth year of his age. It was found after his death that he was in the habit of mortifying himself with a shirt of sackcloth.

La Fontaine was unquestionably the greatest fabulist of his or any other time, and he has been exceedingly popular throughout France. His tales and fables and light poems are full of beauty and grace. But we cannot speak highly of their morality. They are, like almost all French literature, corrupt. They took their character from the times, and have had a bad influence upon later generations of France.

THE INFIDEL.

Perhaps no man has existed in the past history of France, who has had such a wonderful influence over succeeding generations, as Voltaire. I name him the *infidel*, not because his infidelity was the most prominent characteristic, but because he is known more widely in America for his scoffing skepticism. The effect of Voltaire's skeptical writings is more perceptible in Paris than in the provinces, but in the capital an amount of infidelity obtains which is perfectly frightful; and even among those who frequent the church, and sometimes ostentatiously parade an affection for it, this skepticism fills the intellects. No one writer of past years unsettled the already shallow-rooted faith of the people to such an extent as Voltaire. Yet he was by no means the man many of his enemies suppose him to have been. No mere scoffer or reviler of the bible could have obtained such an influence in France as Voltaire did. He was really a great man, and gained the affections of the people by his advocacy of liberty. It is more than probable that under a system of religion as pure as now exists in America, Voltaire would never have been an infidel. The condition of the Catholic church in France, in his time, was sufficiently shocking to have startled every intelligent mind into skepticism. It was filled with hypocrites and knaves, who professed to be filled with the spirit of God, but who in reality were very sensual and wicked men. The slightest independence in religious opinions was punished by exile or imprisonment. How could a man with an independent intellect succumb to such a church? And was it not very natural for it to jump from belief to infidelity? This should be borne in mind when we estimate the character of Voltaire.

Voltaire's real name was Francois-Marie Arouet, and he was born at Chatenay, on the 20th of February, 1694. His father was a notary, and had a lucrative situation. His mother was of noble extraction. When a babe, he was so feeble that it was not expected he would live. An abbe in the family educated him, and it is a singular fact, that when he was a boy, a deistical ode was put into his hands. He entered the college of Louis-le-Grand, and his talents rendered him a general favorite with the teachers. One of his tutors, however, in a religious argument found himself so incompetent to defend the Catholic church, that in his anger he exclaimed, "You will become the Coryphæus of Deism."

On leaving college the young man entered into Paris society. Louis XIV. was in his dotage, and at this time paid little attention to men of genius. Arouet soon became popular in the highest circles for his wit and genius. He resolved, much against his father's will, to devote himself to a literary life. One of the first acts of the young man was to fall in love with a rich but desperate woman's daughter, and amid much opposition he by stealth kept up an intercourse with her; but he was at last obliged to give way before so much ill will. His father was very angry with him—so much so, that he consented at last to study the law. He entered a law-office in Paris, and pursued his studies with industry. He frequented society, but he could not content himself with the prospect of an attorney's life. He beseeched his father to release him from his course of study, and he consented that he should return to the country-seat of a friend, and consider the matter. Here Arouet found a large library, and fed upon it. He staid there until the death of the king, when he went up to Paris to witness the joy of the people. Some verses were printed which were attributed to him, and he was instantly thrown into the Bastille. He passed a year in prison, without society, books, or pen and ink.

While imprisoned, the idea occurred to him of writing a great French epic, and he actually composed in his dungeon two cantos of it, which afterwards were not altered. The poem was called "*Henriade*," and was regarded with admiration by his cotemporaries.

Arouet was finally set free, his innocence being satisfactorily proved. He now issued the tragedy of "*Œdipus*," which had a great success. This success was only deserved in part. He still later wrote several letters upon the tragedies of Sophocles, which gave him at once a high position as a man of learning, and as a critic. His life alternated between work and pleasure. He quarreled with Rosseau about this time, and a little later visited England. He remained away from France three years. Upon his return to Paris he again brought out plays, and was everywhere admired and worshiped. But the priesthood hated him.

He now bought the small estate of Voltaire, and took the name for his own, as was customary at that time. His writings occasionally made light of religion and the priests, and scoffed at their practices. An actress in Paris was refused the rites of burial by the priests, beeause of her life and profession. Voltaire thereupon wrote her apotheosis, and in consequence was obliged to conceal himself for several months in a little village in Normandy. When it was safe for him to emerge from his retirement, he wrote a book on England, which raised another storm about his head. He spoke too highly of English liberty in religious matters, and took occasion to speak sarcastically of all religion. The volume was burned in public, and Voltaire concealed himself in the country.

He now retired to the house of Madam du Chatelet in the country, where he remained for several years. She was a woman of fine intellect, but a harsh nature, and worshipped Voltaire. He here wrote several plays; labored at his essay "*On the Manners and Spirit of Nations;*" collected materials for his "*History of the Age of Louis XIV;*" and wrote the famous "*Pucelle d' Orleans.*" It was while at this house that Voltaire commenced the celebrated correspondence with Frederick the Great. Each had the highest admiration for the other. The great king wrote to him as follows:

"See in me only, I entreat you, a zealous citizen, a somewhat skeptical philosopher, but a truly faithful friend. For God's sake write to me simply as a man; join with me in despising titles, names, and all exterior splendor."

Voltaire replied; "This is a command after my own heart. *I know not how to treat a king;* but I am quite at my ease with a man whose head and heart are full of love for the human race."

The two men met at Cleave. The king had been very anxious for Voltaire to visit the court of Prussia, but he would not without Madame du Chatelet; and Frederic cared not for the acquaintance of a French court lady. Some time after this, Voltaire was sent on a secret mission to Prussia, and startled Frederic by his sudden appearance. He tried to persuade him to take up his abode with him, but the philosopher would not consent. He sighed for his home, and the applause of a Parisian audience.

He brought out other plays, which were well received A minister dying at this time, who had been a bitter enemy of his, he ventured more boldly before the world. He sought to be elected a member of the Academy. A violent opposition arose. He had fought his enemies to the death, never sparing sarcasm or ridicule, and these things could not be forgotten. He lost his election, but was compensated by the success of a new tragedy, which set all Paris into transports of delight.

He was chosen by the duke de Richelieu to negotiate with the king of Prussia in reference to a treaty. He was honored in the highest degree by Frederic—was fêted, praised, and made as much of as if he had been a king. He succeeded in his negotiations, manifesting great subtlety and tact. He returned to the house of Madame du Chatelet. For a time he lived either here or at Paris—until Madame du Chatelet died, when he went to Paris to spend all his time. He was deeply affected by the death of the only woman he ever loved with sincerity. He propitiated the mistress of Louis XV.—Madame Pompadour—and was appointed to a place in the court; and was also made historiographer of France. Soon after, he was elected a member of the Academy, thus triumphing over his old enemies at last. For a time he sacrificed his manly independence, and was not unlike any other court flatterer. He had a rival in Crebillon; and disgusted with the state of things, he accepted the invitation of Frederic, and made him a visit. He was received with the greatest joy by the monarch—who even kissed the poet's hand in a transport of admiration.

The king's cook awaited his orders when he wished to eat in his own rooms, and the king's coach was ready for him when he would ride. He spent two hours each day in studying with the king, correcting his works, etc. etc He was tempted by so much attention to accept of the king a pension and the office of chamberlain; and was obliged to resign his places at the French court. He wrote to a friend in France:

"How can I forget the barbarous manner with which I have been treated in my own country? You know what I have gone through. I enter port after a storm that has lasted thirty years."

He had a salary of twenty thousand francs for himself, and four thousand for his niece, who bitterly opposed the acceptance of Frederick's offer. She prophesied that in the end it would be his death. He went at work correcting his tragedies and writing new plays. He soon thought he discovered deceit in the king, and learned that he was despotic. The keen remarks of each were treasured up. Voltaire heard from a friend that the king had said of him: "I shall not want him more than a year longer—one squeezes the orange and throws away the peel."

The remark caused him much sorrow. The king also treasured up a remark sarcastically made by Voltaire, which was as follows: "When I correct the royal poems I am washing the king's dirty linen." They soon lost their attachment for each other. Voltaire watched in vain for a way to escape from Prussia. At last it came, and he was once more a free man in Switzerland.

He went into a Protestant region, where there were no Catholics, and bought him a pretty estate, and determined to live in complete independence. Persecution however followed him here, and he took up his abode in a retired part of France. He wrote his "*Encyclopedia*," which was severely condemned. In 1788, in his eighty-fourth year, he returned to Paris, bringing with him a newly-written tragedy. His new life in Paris was not good for him, and he died at the end of May.

This was the man who, in the years that followed him, ruled, as it were, the intellect of Paris and France. He was a mighty man, and the fact that he was bitterly persecuted, gave him a hold upon the sympathies of succeeding generations. The conduct of the church toward him was shameful, and he made the sad mistake of rejecting all religion, the true as well as the false.

His plays and writings abound with shocking sentiments, and some of his writings are exceedingly coarse. These scoffs, coming from an ordinary man, would have wrought little harm; but from the great Voltaire, who was worshiped by the French people, they possessed an astonishing power to work iniquity. A New Englander can scarcely credit his senses in Paris when he finds the estimation in which Voltaire and his writings are held by a vast class of the most intelligent Parisians. In religious America he is regarded as a monster of iniquity; in France as a great poet, philosopher, and advocate of human liberty.

THE GREAT COMIC WRITER.

The place where Moliere, the great comic writer of France, lived in Paris, was pointed out to me one day while near the Rue St. Honoré; and I have often noticed on one of the prominent streets a very neat monument to the memory of the great man. It is a niche, with two Corinthian columns, surmounted by a half-circular pediment, which is richly ornamented. A statue of Moliere is placed in the niche in a sitting posture, and in a meditative mood. In front of the columns on each side, there are allegorical figures—one representing his serious, the other his comic plays. Each bears a scroll which contains—one, his comic plays, arranged in chronological order; and the other, his serious plays, arranged in like manner. The basement is beautifully sculptured. The inscriptions are as follows: "*A. Moliere. Né à Paris, le* 15 *Jauvier*, 1622, *et mort à Paris, le* 17 *Février*, 1673." The monument is over fifty feet in height, and cost one hundred and sixty-eight thousand francs. It was erected in 1844, with a great deal of attendant ceremony when it was finished.

Moliere is one of the names of which France is justly proud, and in Paris his memory is half-worshiped. Not to know him well, would be in the eyes of a Parisian the sure sign of intolerable stupidity. He was the greatest comic writer of France, and perhaps of the world. It will not be out of place, therefore, to give a slight sketch of his life.

The real name of Moliere was Jean Baptiste Poguelin, and he was born in a little house in the Rue St. Honore, in the year 1622. His father was a carpet-furnisher to the king, and he was brought up to the same business by his father. His mother died when he was only ten years old, and his father was left with a large family of children to educate. The boy passed his early days in his father's warehouse, but his grandfather was accustomed to take him often to the play-house, where he listened to some of the great Corneille's plays, to his thorough delight. Thus in his youth, even while a mere boy, the taste for the drama was created. His father at one time remonstrated with the old man for taking the boy thus early to the theater, and asked, "Do you mean to make an actor of him?"

Nothing daunted by this question, the grandfather replied, "Yes, if it please God to make him as good a one as Bellerose"—who was the best tragic actor of that time.

The boy was discontented as he grew older, and panted for knowledge. As he contemplated a life given up to trade, he grew melancholy. He was finally sent as an out-student to the college of Clermont, and afterward to the college of Louis-le-Grand, which was under the direction of the Jesuits. The young prince of Conti was at school at that time. Gassendi, the private tutor to the natural son of a man of fortune, named Chapelle—the son at that time at school with Poguelin—discovered the boy's talents, and taught him the philosophy of Epicurus, and gave him lessons in morals. Another of his fellow-students was one de Bergerac, of fine talents but wild disposition. Chapelle and de Bergerac became afterward distinguished.

As soon as he was through college, Poguelin entered into the king's service as *valet de chambre*, and made the journey with his majesty to Narbonne. After this he studied law in Orleans, and commenced practice in Paris as an advocate. He here became associated with a few friends in getting up a series of plays. The age was one full of enthusiasm for the stage, and plays were enacted upon the stage and off of it, in private circles. The club of young men who acted together for the amusement of their friends, were so successful that they resolved to take to the public stage; and as was the custom, each took ar assumed name. Poguelin assumed the name of Moliere, a name which he immortalized, and by which he was ever afterward known.

His father was very much displeased with his course, and sent a friend to persuade him to relinquish it, but the deputy was so fascinated by Poguelin's acting, that he became a convert to him, and was not fitted to urge the arguments of the father. The family for a time refused in a manner to acknowledge their son, being ashamed of his new profession; but they are now known only through him.

The masters under whom Moliere principally studied were Italians, and he imbibed a love for the Italian comic art. He also read the Spanish comedies, and learned to admire them.

Moliere and his little band left Paris for the provinces. The times were unpropitious, for the wars of the Fronde at that time made the whole country a scene of confusion and danger. They had visited Bordeaux, and were protected by the governor of Guienne. While here, Moliere wrote and brought out a tragedy, which had so poor a success that he gave up tragedy. After a short provincial tour he returned to Paris, and renewed the acquaintance of the prince of Conti. The latter caused Moliere and his fellows to bring out plays at his palace. But Paris was too full of strife, and Moliere went to Lyons, where he wrote and brought out his first comedy, "*L'Etouedi.*" It met with a great success. There is an English translation, entitled "Sir Martin Marplot." The next piece was entitled "*Dêpit Amourex,*" and its genuine humor gave it a fine reputation.

The moral character of Moliere at this time was exceedingly bad. The times were such that a band of players found every temptation before them. The French biographers give an account of some of his "gallantries," but they only lead the reader to feel disgust rather than admiration. That plays written by such a man, and during times which corrupted the whole people, should be pure, one could not expect. Moliere's plays, therefore, bear the same character, in this respect, as all the great performances of authors of France in those and succeeding times. They were altogether loose in their morals.

The company of players were invited to Paynas by the prince of Conti, who was staying there at the time. They acted before him, and Moliere wrote several little interludes for the special amusement of the prince, which were afterward the ground-work of some of his best comedies. The prince was so pleased with the comedian, that he invited him to become his secretary. He declined, but whether from love of comedy, or fear of the prince, we do not know. The prince possessed an awful temper, and actually killed his former secretary by throwing the tongs at him.

Paris at length became more quiet, and Moliere turned his steps toward it. He obtained the protection of the king's brother, was introduced to the king, and obtained permission to establish himself in the capital. There was a rival theater at the Hotel de Bourgogue, at which Corneille's tragedies were played. Moliere and his company acted before Louis XIV. and his mother, in the Louvre. The play was that of "Nicomede," and the success was very great. The play was a tragedy, but Moliere knew very well that they could not rival the other tragedy-theater, in that line; and he therefore introduced the custom that night of concluding a tragedy with a farce. The farce acted was one of his own, and was so well received that the custom was ever after kept up. The company finally settled down in the Palais Royal, which the king had granted them.

The next poem which Moliere wrote and brought out, was aimed at a society of men, including many of the most talented in Paris, called the "*Society of the Hotel de Rambouillet.*" The peculiarities of this society were too ridiculous to describe at this day, and Moliere's comedy, which was aimed at them, was wonderfully successful. Paris at once was in an uproar of laughter, and in the midst of the piece an old man rose in the theater, crying out, "Courage, Moliere; this is a true comedy!"

The next piece was entitled "*Sganarelle,*" and although it was quite successful, it was inferior to those which preceded it. Moliere now tried tragedy, but with no success. It was not his *forté.* He returned to comedy, and brought out a piece entitled "*L'Ecoledes Maris,*" which achieved a brilliant success.

At this time Foquet was the minister of finance, and gave a fête in honor of the king; indeed he entertained the king at his villa. He was in some respects another Cardinal Wolsey, in his magnificence and recklessness of display. Foquet loved a beautiful girl, who rejected him. He discovered that the girl loved the king, and that the passion was reciprocated. In his anger he charged it upon the girl, who ran with the secret to the king. Louis was resolved on the downfall of his minister. The fête took place upon a scale of almost unparalleled splendor. Le Brun painted the scenes, La Fontaine wrote verses for it, and Moliere prepared a ballet for the occasion. The king concealed his wrath at this display of wealth, and very much enjoyed Moliere's amusements; and suggested a new comedy to the comedian, while talking with him at the minister's. Fouquet soon fell.

Moliere was by this time so distinguished that he had troops of friends among the wise, learned, and great. Among the warmest of them was the great Condé, who was always pleased with his society. He told the comedian that he feared to trespass by sending for him on peculiar occasions, and therefore requested him to come to him whenever he had a leisure hour; and at such times he would dismiss all other matters, and give himself up to pleasant conversation. The king invariably defended Moliere. A duke once attacked him, and the king reproved the noble. He still attended to his duties as *valet de chambre* to the king, and was constantly subjected to annoyance on account of his profession. The other officers of the king's chamber would not eat with him, such was their petty meanness and pride. The king determined to give them a lesson, so one morning he addressed Moliere as follows:

"I am told you have short commons here, Moliere, and that the officers of my chamber think you unworthy of sharing their meals. You are probably hungry; I got up with a good appetite. Sit down at that table where they have placed my refreshments." The king sat down with him, and the two went heartily at a fowl. The doors were opened, and the most prominent members of court entered. "You see me," said Louis, "employed in giving Moliere his breakfast, as my people do not find him good enough company for themselves." From this time Moliere had no trouble on the score of treatment from his fellow *valets*.

Everywhere except at court, before this, Moliere was treated with the greatest consideration on account of his brilliant genius. He was intimate with Racine and with Boileau. The story for a time was believed that Moliere married his natural daughter, but it has been proved a falsehood. He became attached to the sister of Madelcine Bejaet, a very witty and graceful woman, and married her; but he soon found that she was too fond of admiration to make him happy. She was coquettish, and without principle, and though Moliere bore with her long, they at length separated. He said: "There is but one sort of love, and those who are more easily satisfied, do not know what true love is."

Moliere went on with the management of his theater, and writing and bringing out new plays. One of them—"*L'Ecole des Femmes*"—was translated and amended into the English by Wycherly, and was altogether more licentious in plot than in the original language. It was very popular in England, but not so much so in France.

The next piece of Moliere's was entitled "*Impromptu de Versailles*," and was written at the command of the king. The king and his courtiers were accustomed to take parts in the ballets in those days, and Louis and his court took parts in the ballets of Moliere's construction. The soldiers who guarded the king were accustomed to go into the theater free. They took up a large space, and Moliere represented his loss to the king, who abolished the privilege. The soldiers were very angry, and the next night they cut the door-keeper to pieces with their swords, and forced their way into the house. Moliere made them a speech, and peace was restored. The king offered to punish with severity the lawless soldiery, but Moliere requested him not to do so, and the new order was ever after obeyed without trouble.

One of his next acts was to hold up to ridicule, in a

comedy, the medical faculty. The condition of the medical art at that time was such that it richly deserved ridicule. But no man can thus attack great bodies of men without making enemies, and Moliere had them without number.

The comedian was now at the height of his prosperity, and still he was unhappy. Separated from his wife, whose conduct was now shameful, he had no domestic happiness. He spent much of his time at his country-house at Antenil, where an apartment was always kept for his old school-fellow, Chapelle, for whom he always retained a warm affection. He was often alone, and preferred solitude, shutting himself away from society. A supper was once given by him to all his brother wits. He alone was indisposed, and as he took no wine or animal food, he went early to bed, leaving his friends merry over their wine. At last they grew so affected by the wine they had drank, that they were ready to follow a leader into any absurdity. Chapelle was, when tipsy, always melancholy, and on this occasion he addressed his companions in a strain of bathos which, had they been free from the effects of wine, would only have excited their laughter. But now they were in the same condition as himself. Chapelle finally wound up by proposing that they all proceed to a neighboring river, and end life together by plunging into it. He expiated upon the heroism of the act, and the immortality it would give them, and they all agreed to it. Moliere overheard them quitting the house, and suspecting something wrong, followed them. He came up with them upon the bank of the river, when they besought him alsc to die with them. He professed to be struck with the heroism of their plan, but demanded that it should be executed in the broad day. They fell in with his suggestion, and returned to the house. Of course, the next morning they were ashamed to look upon each other's faces.

Moliere wrote many new plays and farces, but his days were fast drawing to a close. He was overworked, and took little care of his health. The king asked him one day what he did with his doctor. "We converse together," he replied—"he writes prescriptions, which I do not take, and I recover." He had a weak chest, and a constant cough.

About this time his friends persuaded him to invite his wife again to his house, and she urged him to a more generous diet, but he grew the worse for it. He now brought out a new play, and could not be prevented from taking a prominent part in it. On the fourth night he was much worse, and friends gathered around him, beseeching him not to go on the stage longer. He replied, "There are fifty poor workmen whose bread depends on the daily receipts. I should reproach myself if I deprived them of it." But while making others laugh, he was actually dying. He was, while in the ballet, seized with a fit of coughing, and burst a blood-vessel. A priest was sent for, but such was their antipathy to the comedian, that it was long before one could be found willing to attend him. He expired with but few friends around him. Two sisters of charity whom he had been in the habit of receiving in his house while they were collecting alms during Lent, remembered his generosity, and attended his death-bed.

The archbishop of Paris refused the rites of burial to the body. His wife was much moved by this act, and exclaimed, "What! refuse burial to one who deserves that altars should be erected to him!" She ran to the king, who being offended by some indiscretion of hers, refused to interfere in the matter, though he privately ordered the archbishop to take off the interdiction. When the funeral took place, a mob of low people, excited by their priestly advisers, attended, intending to offer insult to the body, but the comedian's widow propitiated them by throwing a thousand francs among them. We see by this shameful treatment of a man whom France honored, and who, though not irreproachable in character, was as pure as those who persecuted him.

Moliere was almost universally honored—always excepting those bodies which he had ridiculed. He was very generous, and would, long before his death, have given up acting on the stage, were it not for his companions whose subsistence depended upon his appearance with them.

Very many years after, the eulogy of Moliere was made the subject of a prize; and when it was delivered, two persons by the name of Poguelin were honored by a seat on the stage.

At his death the band of comedians was broken up. His widow received a pension, in after years, of one thousand livres. But one of his children survived, and that one had no issue—so the race soon became extinct.

THE END.

www.ingramcontent.com/pod-product-compliance
Lightning Source LLC
LaVergne TN
LVHW020234110826
845151LV00003B/922